Britain in Verse

Designed by Robert Mathias, Publishing Workshop
Line illustrations by Brian Pearce

Published 1985 by
The Hamlyn Publishing Group Limited,
a Division of the Octopus Publishing Group plc,
Michelin House, 81 Fulham Road, London SW3 6RB.

Second impression 1988

Printed in Italy

ISBN 0 600 30635 6

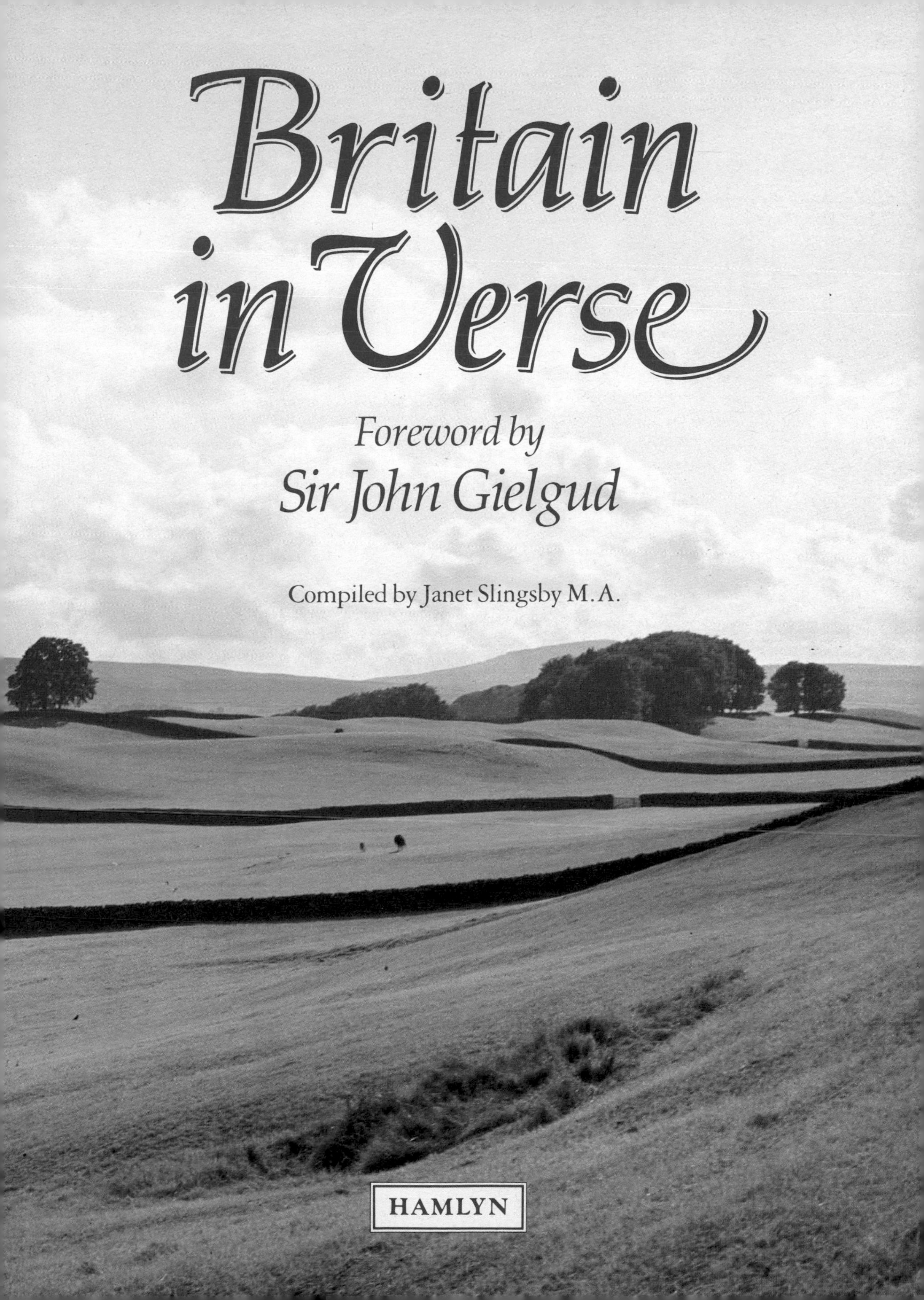

Britain in Verse

Foreword by

Sir John Gielgud

Compiled by Janet Slingsby M.A.

HAMLYN

Foreword

I confess to having read shamefully little poetry when I was a young man; though, as I was stage-struck at a very early age, I soon began to read Shakespeare with love and enthusiasm, and even learned many of his scenes and poems which have delighted me ever since.

During the last thirty years or so, however, I have read a good deal of great poetry, much of it aloud, both on the stage, in television and radio programmes, and in church, and I was pleasantly surprised to find so many pieces familiar to me in the delightful anthology which I have been asked to preface. Some of the poems, however, are quite new to me and they will act as an encouragement to pursue my belated attempts to enjoy in fuller measure the great variety of verse which our beautiful countryside has inspired.

An aptly-selected anthology is always a varied and comparatively easy diversion: not only am I an impatient and often careless reader, but I find it very difficult to concentrate in reading one very long poem. For me, there is always the same danger as in listening to classical music when I am all too often lulled by the flow and rhythm to the exclusion of a detailed apprehension of sense and meaning; though, of course, in many of the great Shakespearian speeches, as Bernard Shaw remarked, the sound can often express the mood and emotions of the poet as clearly and powerfully as the exact meaning of the words, in the famous speeches of *The Tempest* for instance, and in *Antony and Cleopatra*.

I suppose that a poet or composer must examine his work with quite a different eye from that of the person who reads or listens to it. But, of course, the moment an actor has to read poetry aloud, he is forced to pay the utmost attention to the writer's art in every facet – correct pronunciation, phrasing, tempo – and one finds continually new and fascinating details in a work which one has so often failed to appreciate in a more perfunctory reading.

Poetry, like music, has obviously a very individual effect upon every reader. Even in the theatre, when the actor is trying to elicit a response from a mass audience, the reactions of the listeners are bound to vary to an extraordinary degree. In an imaginative performance, it is even possible to convey an effect which one had no idea of oneself. It is a rare privilege to discover, in one's old age, some of the secrets that a close familiarity with poetry can so magically reveal. I feel sure that this enchanting book will find the same enthusiastic appreciation for other readers as it has had for me.

John Gielgud

Contents

Part One

'Every Changing Season'

'And every changing season of the year
Stamps on the scene its English character.'

English Character

George Crabbe

How stately stand yon pines upon the hill,
How soft the murmurs of that living rill,
And o'er the park's tall paling, scarcely higher,
Peeps the low Church and shows the modest spire.
Unnumber'd violets on those banks appear,
And all the first-born beauties of the year,
The grey-green blossoms of the willow bring
The large wild bees upon the labouring wing.
Then comes the Summer with augmented pride,
Whose pure small streams along the valleys glide:
Her richer Flora their brief charms display;
And, as the fruit advances, fall away.
Then shall th' autumnal yellow clothe the leaf,
What time the reaper binds the burden'd sheaf;
Then silent groves denote the dying year,
The morning frost, the noon-tide gossamer;
And all be silent in the scene around,
All save the distant sea's uncertain sound,
Or here and there the gun whose loud report
Proclaims to man that Death is but his sport;
And then the wintry winds begin to blow,
Then fall the flaky stars of gathering snow,
When on the thorn the ripening sloe, yet blue,
Takes the bright varnish of the morning dew;
The aged moss grows brittle on the pale,
The dry boughs splinter on the windy gale,
And every changing season of the year
Stamps on the scene its English character.

The Months of the Year

Sara Coleridge

January brings the snow;
Makes the toes and fingers glow.

February brings the rain,
Thaws the frozen ponds again.

March brings breezes loud and shrill,
Stirs the dancing daffodil.

April brings the primrose sweet,
Scatters daisies at our feet.

May brings flocks of pretty lambs,
Skipping by their fleecy dams.

June brings tulips, lilies, roses;
Fills the children's hands with posies.

Hot July brings cooling showers,
Strawberries and gilly-flowers.

August brings the sheaves of corn,
Then the Harvest home is borne.

Warm September brings the fruit,
Sportsmen then begin to shoot.

Fresh October brings the pheasant;
Then to gather nuts is pleasant.

Dull November brings the blast,
Then the leaves are falling fast.

Chill December brings the sleet,
Blazing fire and Christmas treat.

Winter

(*from* Love's Labour's Lost)

William Shakespeare

When icicles hang by the wall,
And Dick the shepherd blows his nail,
And Tom bears logs into the hall,
And milk comes frozen home in pail,
When blood is nipp'd, and ways be foul,
Then nightly sings the staring owl,
Tu-who;
Tu-whit, tu-who–a merry note,
While greasy Joan doth keel the pot.

When all aloud the wind doth blow,
And coughing drowns the parson's saw,
And birds sit brooding in the snow,
And Marian's nose looks red and raw,
When roasted crabs hiss in the bowl,
Then nightly sings the staring owl,
Tu-who;
Tu-whit, tu-who–a merry note,
While greasy Joan doth keel the pot.

A Frosty Day

Lord de Tabley

Grass afield wears silver thatch;
Palings all are edged with rime;
Frost-flowers pattern round the latch;
Cloud nor breeze dissolve the clime:

When the waves are solid floor,
And the clods are iron-bound,
And the boughs are crystall'd hoar,
And the red leaf nailed aground.

When the fieldfare's flight is slow,
And a rosy vapour rim,
Now the sun is small and low,
Belts along the region dim.

When the ice-crack flies and flaws,
  Shore to shore, with thunder shock,
Deeper then the evening daws,
  Clearer than the village clock.

When the rusty blackbird strips,
  Bunch by bunch, the coral thorn;
And the pale day-crescent dips,
  New to heaven, a slender horn.

Snow

Walter de la Mare

No breath of wind,
No gleam of sun –
Still the white snow
Whirls softly down –
Twig and bough
And blade and thorn
All in an icy
Quiet, forlorn.
Whispering, rustling,
Through the air,
On sill and stone,
Roof – everywhere,
It heaps its powdery
Crystal flakes,
Of every tree
A mountain makes;
Till pale and faint
At shut of day,
Stoops from the West
One wintry ray.
And, feathered in fire,
Where ghosts the moon,
A robin shrills
His lonely tune.

At Middle-Field Gate in February

Thomas Hardy

The bars are thick with drops that show
   As they gather themselves from the fog
Like silver buttons ranged in a row,
And as evenly spaced as if measured, although
   They fall at the feeblest jog.

They load the leafless hedge hard by,
   And the blades of last year's grass,
While the fallow ploughland turned up nigh
In raw rolls, clammy and clogging lie –
   Too clogging for feet to pass.

How dry it was on a far-back day
   When straws hung the hedge and around,
When amid the sheaves in amorous play
In curtained bonnets and light array
   Bloomed a bevy now underground!

Thaw

Edward Thomas

Over the land freckled with snow half-thawed
The speculating rooks at their nests cawed
And saw from elm-tops, delicate as flower of grass,
What we below could not see, Winter pass.

A Dream of the Unknown

Percy Bysshe Shelley

I dream'd that as I wander'd by the way
   Bare Winter suddenly was changed to Spring,
And gentle odours led my steps astray,
   Mix'd with a sound of waters murmuring
Along a shelving bank of turf, which lay
   Under a copse, and hardly dared to fling
Its green arms round the bosom of the stream,
But kiss'd it and then fled, as Thou mightest in dream.

There grew pied wind-flowers and violets,
   Daisies, those pearl'd Arcturi of the earth,
The constellated flower that never sets;
   Faint oxlips; tender blue-bells, at whose birth
The sod scarce heaved; and that tall flower that wets
It's mother's face with heaven-collected tears,
When the low wind, its playmate's voice, it hears.

And in the warm hedge grew lush eglantine,
   Green cow-bind and the moonlight-colour'd May,
And cherry-blossoms, and white cups, whose wine
   Was the bright dew yet drain'd not by the day;
And wild roses, and ivy serpentine
   With its dark buds and leaves, wandering astray;
And flowers azure, black, and streak'd with gold,
Fairer than any waken'd eyes behold.

And nearer to the river's trembling edge
   There grew broad flag-flowers, purple prank't with white,
And starry river-buds among the sedge,
   And floating water-lilies, broad and bright,
Which lit the oak that overhung the hedge
   With moonlight beams of their own watery light;
And bulrushes, and reeds of such deep green
As soothed the dazzled eye with sober sheen.

Methought that of these visionary flowers
   I made a nosegay, bound in such a way
That the same hues, which in their natural bowers
   Were mingled or opposed, the like array
Kept these imprison'd children of the Hours
   Within my hand, – and then, elate and gay,
I hasten'd to the spot whence I had come
That I might there present it – O! to Whom?

Home-Thoughts, from Abroad

Robert Browning

Oh, to be in England
Now that April's there,
And whoever wakes in England
Sees, some morning, unaware,
That the lowest boughs and the brushwood sheaf
Round the elm-tree bole are in tiny leaf,
While the chaffinch sings on the orchard bough
In England – now!
And after April, when May follows,
And the whitethroat builds, and all the swallows!
Hark, where my blossomed pear-tree in the hedge
Leans to the field and scatters on the clover
Blossoms and dewdrops – at the bent spray's edge –
That's the wise thrush; he sings each song twice over,
Lest you should think he never could recapture
The first fine careless rapture!
And though the fields look rough with hoary dew,
All will be gay when noontide wakes anew
The buttercups, the little children's dower
– Far brighter than this gaudy melon-flower!

The Ecchoing Green

William Blake

The Sun does arise,
And make happy the skies;
The merry bells ring
To welcome the Spring;
The sky-lark and thrush,
The birds of the bush,
Sing louder around
To the bells' chearful sound,
While our sports shall be seen
On the Ecchoing Green.

Old John with white hair,
Does laugh away care,
Sitting under the oak
Among the old folk.
They laugh at our play,
And soon they all say:
'Such, such were the joys
When we all, girls & boys,
In our youth-time were seen
On the Ecchoing Green.'

Till the little ones, weary,
No more can be merry;
The sun does descend,
And our sports have an end.
Round the laps of their mothers
Many sisters and brothers,
Like birds in their nest,
Are ready for rest,
And sport no more seen
On the darkening Green.

Weathers

Thomas Hardy

This is the weather the cuckoo likes,
   And so do I;
When showers betumble the chestnut spikes,
   And nestlings fly;
And the little brown nightingale bills his best,
And they sit outside at 'The Travellers' Rest',
And maids come forth sprig-muslin drest,
And citizens dream of the south and west,
   And so do I.

This is the weather the shepherd shuns,
   And so do I;
When beeches drip in browns and duns,
   And thresh, and ply;
And hill-hid tides throb, throe on throe,
And meadow rivulets overflow,
And drops on gate-bars hang in a row,
And rooks in families homeward go,
   And so do I.

The Orchard

William Barnes

Within the orchard's many shadows,
   Flitting softly round our feet.
While burning hot, the sunlight shot
   Between them in the summer heat;
We went, at times, by dock-leaves, falling
Limp, beside the mossy walling.

The way from garden into orchard
   Through an arched gateway led,
Where rose a dovecote up above
   The grey old arch, above the head,
By flower-beds of the oldest fashion,
Sweet with rose and red carnation.

There spreading trees of mossy oldness,
 This and that way leaning lay;
And others, young and upright, sprung
 For year-stunn'd old ones cast away;
Within a thorny hedge that girded
Ground, and tree bough, many birded.

There shone the boughs, in May's gay sunshine,
 Out in blooth as white's a sheet;
Or else their flowers fell in showers
 Softly down about their feet;
Or else they nodded, many-appled,
Green, or lastly ruddy-dappled.

And then the time of apple-taking
 Came, and apples pattered down
Below the trees, in twos and threes,
 Full thick; and yellow, red and brown,
To folks that filled, from baskets by them,
Bags as full as they could tie them.

A Bay in Anglesey

John Betjeman

The sleepy sound of a tea-time tide
Slaps at the rocks the sun has dried,

Too lazy, almost, to sink and lift
Round low peninsulas pink with thrift.

The water, enlarging shells and sand,
Grows greener emerald out from land

And brown over shadowy shelves below
The waving forests of seaweed show.

Here at my feet in the short cliff grass
Are shells, dried bladderwrack, broken glass,

Pale blue squills and yellow rock roses.
The next low ridge that we climb discloses

One more field for the sheep to graze
While, scarcely seen on this hottest of days,

Far to the eastward, over there,
Snowdon rises in pearl-grey air.

Multiple lark-song, whispering bents,
The thymy, turfy and salty scents

And filling in, brimming in, sparkling and free
The sweet susurration of incoming sea.

Haymaking

Edward Thomas

After night's thunder far away had rolled
The fiery day had a kernel sweet of cold,
And in the perfect blue the clouds uncurled,
Like the first gods before they made the world
And misery, swimming the stormless sea
In beauty and in divine gaiety.
The smooth white empty road was lightly strewn
With leaves – the holly's Autumn falls in June –
And fir cones standing stiff up in the heat.
The mill-foot tumbled white and lit
With tossing crystals, happier than any crowd
Of children pouring out of school aloud.
And in the little thickets where a sleeper
For ever might lie lost, the nettle-creeper
And garden warbler sang unceasingly;
While over them shrill shrieked in his fierce glee
The swift with wings and tail as sharp and narrow
As if the bow had flown off with the arrow.
Only the scent of woodbine and hay new-mown
Travelled the road. In the fields sloping down,
Park-like, to where its willows showed the brook,
Haymakers rested. The tosser lay forsook

Out in the sun; and the long waggon stood
Without its team, it seemed it never would
Move from the shadow of that single yew.
The team, as still, until their task was due,
Beside the labourers enjoyed the shade
That three squat oaks mid-field together made
Upon a circle of grass and weed uncut,
And on the hollow, once a chalk-pit, but
Now brimmed with nut and elder-flower so clean,
The men leaned on their rakes, about to begin,
But still. And all were silent. All was old,
This morning time, with a great age untold,
Older than Clare and Cobbett, Morland and Crome,
Than, at the field's far edge, the farmer's home,
A white house crouched at the foot of a great tree.
Under the heavens that know not what years be
The men, the beasts, the trees, the implements
Uttered even what they will in times far hence –
All of us gone out of the reach of change –
Immortal in a picture of an old grange.

The Hock-cart or Harvest Home. To the Right Honourable Mildmay, Earl of Westmoreland

Robert Herrick

Come, sons of summer, by whose toil
We are the lords of wine and oil:
By whose tough labours and rough hands
We rip up first, then reap our lands.
Crown'd with the ears of corn, now come,
And to the pipe sing harvest home.
Come forth, my lord, and see the cart
Dress'd up with all the country art:
See here a maukin, there a sheet,
As spotless pure as it is sweet:
The horses, mares, and frisking fillies,
Clad all in linen white as lilies.
The harvest swains and wenches bound
For joy, to see the hock-cart crown'd.

About the cart, hear how the rout
Of rural younglings raise the shout;
Pressing before, some coming after,
Those with a shout, and these with laughter.
Some bless the cart, some kiss the sheaves,
Some prank them up with oaken leaves:
Some cross the fill-horse, some with great
Devotion stroke the home-borne wheat:
While other rustics, less attent
To prayers than to merriment,
Run after with their breeches rent.
Well, on, brave boys, to your lord's hearth,
Glitt'ring with fire, where, for your mirth,
Ye shall see first the large and chief
Foundation of your feast, fat beef:
With upper stories, mutton, veal
And bacon (which makes full the meal),
With sev'ral dishes standing by,
As here a custard, there a pie,
And here all-tempting frumenty.
And for to make the merry cheer,
If smirking wine be wanted here,
There's that which drowns all care, stout beer;
Which freely drink to your lord's health,
Then to the plough, the commonwealth,
Next to your flails, your fans, your fats,
Then to the maids with wheaten hats:
To the rough sickle, and crook'd scythe,
Drink, frolic boys, till all be blithe.
Feed, and grow fat; and as ye eat
Be mindful that the lab'ring neat,
As you, may have their fill of meat.
And know, besides, ye must revoke
The patient ox unto the yoke,
And all go back unto the plough
And harrow, though they're hang'd up now.
And, you must know, your lord's word's true,
Feed him ye must, whose food fills you;
And that this pleasure is like rain,
Not sent ye for to drown your pain,
But for to make it spring again.

Poem in October

Dylan Thomas

It was my thirtieth year to heaven
Woke to my hearing from harbour and neighbour wood
And the mussel pooled and the heron
Priested shore
The morning beckon
With water praying and call of seagull and rook
And the knock of sailing boats on the net webbed wall
Myself to set foot
That second
In the still sleeping town and set forth.

My birthday began with the water-
Birds and the birds of the winged trees flying my name
Above the farms and the white horses
And I rose
In rainy autumn
And walked abroad in a shower of all my days.
High tide and the heron dived when I took the road
Over the border
And the gates
Of the town closed as the town awoke.

A springful of larks in a rolling
Cloud and the roadside bushes brimming with whistling
Blackbirds and the sun of October
Summery
On the hill's shoulder,
Here were fond climates and sweet singers suddenly
Come in the morning where I wandered and listened
To the rain wringing
Wind blow cold
In the wood faraway under me.

Pale rain over the dwindling harbour
And over the sea wet church the size of a snail
With its horns through mist and the castle
Brown as owls
But all the gardens

Of spring and summer were blooming in the tall tales
Beyond the border and under the lark full cloud.
There could I marvel
My birthday
Away but the weather turned around.

It turned away from the blithe country
And down the other air and the blue altered sky
Streamed again a wonder of summer
With apples
Pears and red currants
And I saw in the turning so clearly a child's
Forgotten mornings when he walked with his mother
Through the parables
Of sun light
And the legends of the green chapels

And the twice told fields of infancy
That his tears burned my cheeks and his heart moved in mine.
These were the woods the river and sea
Where a boy
In the listening
Summertime of the dead whispered the truth of his joy
To the trees and the stones and the fish in the tide.
And the mystery
Sang alive
Still in the water and singingbirds.

And there could I marvel my birthday
Away but the weather turned around. And the true
Joy of the long dead child sang burning
In the sun.
It was my thirtieth
Year to heaven stood there then in the summer noon
Though the town below lay leaved with October blood.
O may my heart's truth
Still be sung
On this high hill in a year's turning.

To Autumn

John Keats

Season of mists and mellow fruitfulness,
Close bosom-friend of the maturing sun;
Conspiring with him how to load and bless
With fruit the vines that round the thatch-eves run;
To bend with apples the moss'd cottage-trees,
And fill all fruit with ripeness to the core;
To swell the gourd, and plump the hazel shells
With a sweet kernel; to set budding more,
And still more, later flowers for the bees,
Until they think warm days will never cease,
For Summer has o'er-brimm'd their clammy cells.

Who hath not seen thee oft amid thy store?
Sometimes whoever seeks abroad may find
Thee sitting careless on a granary floor,
Thy hair soft-lifted by the winnowing wind;
Or on a half-reap'd furrow sound asleep,
Drows'd with the fume of poppies, while thy hook
Spares the next swath and all its twined flowers:
And sometimes like a gleaner thou dost keep
Steady thy laden head across a brook;
Or by a cyder-press, with patient look,
Thou watchest the last oozings hours by hours.

Where are the songs of Spring? Ay, where are they?
Think not of them, thou has thy music too, –
While barred clouds bloom the soft-dying day,
And touch the stubble-plains with rosy hue;
Then in a wailful choir the small gnats mourn
Among the river sallows, borne aloft
Or sinking as the light wind lives or dies;
And full-grown lambs loud bleat from hilly bourn;
Hedge-crickets sing; and now with treble soft
The red-breast whistles from a garden-croft;
And gathering swallows twitter in the skies.

Autumn

Thomas Hood

I saw old Autumn in the misty morn
Stand shadowless like Silence, listening
To silence, for no lonely bird would sing
Into his hollow ear from woods forlorn,
Nor lowly hedge nor solitary thorn;
Shaking his languid locks all dewy bright
With tangled gossamer that fell by night,
   Pearling his coronet of golden corn.

Where are the songs of Summer? – With the sun,
Oping the dusky eyelids of the south,
Till shade and silence waken up as one,
And Morning sings with a warm odorous mouth.
Where are the merry birds? – Away, away,
On panting wings through the inclement skies,
   Lest owls should prey
   Undazzled at noonday,
And tear with horny beak their lustrous eyes.

Where are the blooms of Summer? – In the west,
Blushing their last to the last sunny hours,
When the mild Eve by sudden Night is prest
Like tearful Proserpine, snatch'd from her flow'rs
   To a most gloomy breast.
Where is the pride of Summer, – the green prime, –
The many, many leaves all twinkling? – Three
   On the mossed elm; three on the naked lime
Trembling, – and one upon the old oak tree!
   Where is the Dryads' immortality?
Gone into mournful cypress and dark yew,
Or wearing the long gloomy Winter through
   In the smooth holly's green eternity.

The squirrel gloats on his accomplished hoard,
The ants have brimmed their garners with ripe grain,
   And honey bees have stored
The sweets of Summer in their luscious cells;
The swallows all have wing'd across the main;

But here the Autumn melancholy dwells,
And sighs her tearful spells,
Amongst the sunless shadows of the plain.
        Alone, alone,
        Upon a mossy stone,
She sits and reckons up the dead and gone
With the last leaves for a love-rosary,
Whilst all the wither'd world looks drearily,
Like a dim picture of the drowned past
In the hush'd mind's mysterious far away
Doubtful what ghostly thing will steal the last
Into that distance, grey upon the grey.

O go and sit with her, and be o'ershaded
Under thc languid downfall of her hair:
She wears a coronal of flowers faded
Upon her forehead, and a face of care;
There is enough of wither'd everywhere
To make her bower, – and enough of gloom;
There is enough of sadness to invite,
If only for the rose that died, – whose doom
Is Beauty's, – she that with the living bloom
Of conscious cheeks most beautifies the light:
There is enough of sorrowing, and quite
Enough of bitter fruits the earth doth bear, –
Enough of chilly droppings for her bowl;
Enough of fear and shadowy despair,
To frame her cloudy prison for the soul!

Part Two

'A Goodly Prospect'

'Heavens! what a goodly prospect spreads around,
Of hills, and dales, and woods, and lawns, and spires,
And glittering towns, and gilded streams, till all
The stretching landscape into smoke decays!
Happy Britannia!'

Britannia

James Thomson

Heavens! what a goodly prospect spreads around,
Of hills, and dales, and woods, and lawns, and spires,
And glittering towns, and gilded streams, till all
The stretching landscape into smoke decays!
Happy Britannia! where, the Queens of Arts
Inspiring vigour, liberty abroad
Walks, unconfined, e'en to thy farthest cots,
And scatters plenty with unsparing hand.
Rich is thy soil, and merciful thy clime;
Thy streams unfailing in the summer's drought;
Unmatched thy guardian oaks; thy valleys float
With golden waves: and, on thy mountains flocks
Bleat numberless; while, roving round their sides,
Bellow the blackening herds in lusty droves.
Beneath, thy meadows glow, and rise unquelled
Against the mower's scythe. On every hand
Thy villas shine. Thy country teems with wealth;
And property assures it to the swain,
Pleased and unwearied, in his guarded toil.

from John of Gaunt's Speech

(*from* Richard II)

William Shakespeare

This royal throne of kings, this sceptered isle,
This earth of majesty, this seat of Mars,
This other Eden, demi-paradise;
This fortress built by Nature for herself
Against infection and the hand of war;
This happy breed of men, this little world;
This precious stone set in the silver sea,
Which serves it in the office of a wall,
Or as a moat defensive to a house,
Against the envy of less happier lands;
This blessed plot, this earth, this realm, this England . . .

Zennor

Anne Ridler

Seen from these cliffs the sea circles slowly.
  Ponderous and blue today, with waves furled,
  Slowly it crosses the curved world.
We wind in its waters with the tide,
  But the pendent ships afar
  Where the lightest blue and low clouds are
We lose as they hover and over the horizon slide.

When it was a dark blue heaven with foam like stars
  We saw it lean above us from the shore,
  And over the rocks the waves rear
Immense, and coming in with crests on fire;
  We could not understand,
  Finding the sea so high above the land,
What held its waters from flooding the world entire.

Today it lies in place, and the dun houses,
  The apple-green cloudy oats, the cows that seem
  Compact of the yellow crust of their cream,
Shrink on Amalveor's grey and tawny sides,
  Sucking the last shreds of sun.
  But all life here is carried on
Against the crash and cry of the moving tides.

Trebetherick

John Betjeman

We used to picnic where the thrift
Grew deep and tufted to the edge;
We saw the yellow foam-flakes drift
In trembling sponges on the ledge
Below us, till the wind would lift
Them up the cliff and o'er the hedge.
Sand in the sandwiches, wasps in the tea,
Sun on our bathing-dresses heavy with the wet,
Squelch of the bladder-wrack waiting for the sea,
Fleas round the tamarisk, an early cigarette.

From where the coastguard houses stood
One used to see, below the hill,
The lichened branches of a wood
In summer silver-cool and still;
And there the Shade of Evil could
Stretch out at us from Shilla Mill.
Thick with sloe and blackberry, uneven in the light,
Lonely ran the hedge, the heavy meadow was remote,
The oldest part of Cornwall was the wood as black as night,
And the pheasant and the rabbit lay torn open at the throat.

But when a storm was at its height,
And feathery slate was black in rain,
And tamarisks were hung with light
And golden sand was brown again,
Spring tide and blizzard would unite
And sea came flooding up the lane.
Waves full of treasure then were roaring up the beach,
Ropes round our mackintoshes, waders warm and dry,
We waited for the wreckage to come swirling into reach,
Ralph, Vasey, Alastair, Biddy, John and I.

Then roller into roller curled
And thundered down the rocky bay,
And we were in a water-world
Of rain and blizzard, sea and spray,
And one against the other hurled

We struggled round to Greenaway.
Blesséd be St. Enodoc, blesséd be the wave,
Blesséd be the springy turf, we pray, pray to thee,
Ask for our children all the happy days you gave
To Ralph, Vasey, Alastair, Biddy, John and me.

from DEVONSHIRE SCENES

Coventry Patmore

I cross'd the furze-grown table-land,
  And near'd the northern vales,
That lay perspicuously plann'd
  In lesser hills and dales.
Then rearward, in a slow review,
  Fell Dartmoor's jagged lines;
Around were dross-heaps, red and blue,
  Old shafts of gutted mines,
Impetuous currents copper-stain'd,
  Wheels stream-urged with a roar,
Sluice-guiding grooves, strong works that strain'd
  With freight of upheaved ore.
And then, the train, with shock on shock,
  Swift rush and birth-scream dire,
Grew from the bosom of the rock,
  And pass'd in noise and fire.
With brazen throb, with vital stroke,
  It went, far heard, far seen,
Setting a track of shining smoke
  Against the pastoral green.
Then, bright drops, lodged in budding trees,
  Were loos'd in sudden showers,
Touch'd by the novel western breeze,
  Friend of the backward flowers.
Then rose the Church at Tavistock,
  The rain still falling there;
But sunny Dartmoor seem'd to mock
  The gloom with cheerful glare.
About the West the gilt vane reel'd
  And pois'd; and, with sweet art,
The sudden, jangling changes peal'd.
  Until, around my heart,
Conceits of brighter times, of times
  The brighter for past storms,
Clung thick as bees, when brazen chimes
  Call down the hiveless swarms.

I rested at the Tiger Inn,
   There half-way on my ride,
And mused with joy of friends and kin
   Who did my coming bide.
The Vicar, in his sombre wear
   That shone about the knees,
Before me stood, his aspect fair
   With godly memories.
I heard again his kind 'Good-bye:
   Christ speed and keep thee still
From frantic passions, for they die
   And leave a frantic will.'
My fond, old Tutor, learn'd and meek!
   A soul, in strangest truth,
As wide as Asia and as weak;
   Not like his daughter Ruth.
A Girl of fullest heart she was;
   Her spirit's lovely flame
Nor dazzled nor surprised, because
   It always burn'd the same;
And in the maiden path she trod
   Fair was the wife foreshown,
A Mary in the house of God,
   A Martha in her own.
Charms for the sight she had; but these
   Were tranquil, grave, and chaste,
And all too beautiful to please
   A rash, untutor'd taste.

In love with home, I rose and eyed
   The rainy North; but there
The distant hill-top, in its pride,
   Adorn'd the brilliant air:
And, as I pass'd from Tavistock,
   The scatter'd dwellings white,
The Church, the golden weather-cock,
   Were whelm'd in happy light;
The children 'gan the sun to greet,
   With song and senseless shout;
The lambs to skip, their dams to bleat;

In Tavy leapt the trout;
Across a fleeting eastern cloud,
The splendid rainbow sprang,
And larks, invisible and loud,
Within its zenith sang.

So lay the Earth that saw the skies
Grow clear and bright above,
As the repentant spirit lies
In God's forgiving love.
The lark forsook the waning day,
And all loud songs did cease;
The Robin, from a wither'd spray,
Sang like a soul at peace.
Far to the South, in sunset glow'd
The peaks of Dartmoor ridge,
And Tamar, full and tranquil, flow'd
Beneath the Gresson Bridge.

This Lime-Tree Bower my Prison

Samuel Taylor Coleridge

Well, they are gone, and here must I remain,
This lime-tree bower my prison! I have lost
Beauties and feelings, such as would have been
Most sweet to my rememberance even when age
Had dimmed mine eyes to blindness! They, meanwhile,
Friends, whom I never more may meet again,
On springy heath, along the hill-top edge,
Wander in gladness, and wind down, perchance,
To that still roaring dell, of which I told;

The roaring dell, o'erwooded, narrow, deep,
And only speckled by the mid-day sun;
Where its slim trunk the ash from rock to rock
Flings arching like a bridge; – that branchless ash,
Unsunned and damp, whose few poor yellow leaves
Ne'er tremble in the gale, yet tremble still,
Fanned by the water-fall! and there my friends
Behold the dark green file of long lank weeds,
That all at once (a most fantastic sight!)
Still nod and drip beneath the dripping edge
Of the blue clay-stone.

Now, my friends emerge
Beneath the wide wide Heaven – and view again
The many-steepled tract magnificent
Of hilly fields and meadows, and the sea,
With some fair bark, perhaps, whose sails light up
The slip of smooth clear blue betwixt two Isles
Of purple shadow! Yes! they wander on
In gladness all; but thou, methinks, most glad,
My gentle-hearted Charles! for thou hast pined
And hungered after Nature, many a year,
In the great City pent, winning thy way
With sad yet patient soul, through evil and pain
And strange calamity! Ah! slowly sink
Behind the western ridge, thou glorious sun!
Shine in the slant beams of the sinking orb,
Ye purple heath-flowers! richlier burn, ye clouds!
Live in the yellow light, ye distant groves!
And kindle, thou blue ocean! So my Friend
Struck with deep joy may stand, as I have stood,
Silent with swimming sense; yea, gazing round
On the wide landscape, gaze till all doth seem
Less gross than bodily; and of such hues
As veil the Almighty Spirit, when yet he makes
Spirits perceive his presence.

A delight
Comes sudden on my heart, and I am glad
As I myself were there! Nor in this bower,
This little lime-tree bower, have I not marked
Much that has soothed me. Pale beneath the blaze

Hung the transparent foliage; and I watched
Some broad and sunny leaf, and loved to see
The shadow of the leaf and stem above
Dappling its sunshine! And that walnut-tree
Was richly tinged, and a deep radiance lay
Full on the ancient ivy, which usurps
Those fronting elms, and now, with blackest mass
Makes their dark branches gleam a lighter hue
Through the late twilight: and though now the bat
Wheels silent by, and not a swallow twitters,
Yet still the solitary humble bee
Sings in the bean-flower! Henceforth I shall know
That Nature ne'er deserts the wise and pure;
No plot so narrow, be but Nature there,
No waste so vacant, but may well employ
Each faculty of sense, and keep the heart
Awake to Love and Beauty! and sometimes
'Tis well to be bereft of promised good,
That we may lift the Soul, and contemplate
With lively joy the joys we cannot share.
My gentle-hearted Charles! when the last rook
Beat its straight path along the dusky air
Homewards, I blest it! deeming, its black wing
(Now a dim speck, now vanishing in light)
Had crossed the mighty orb's dilated glory,
While thou stood'st gazing; or when all was still,
Flew creeking o'er thy head, and had a charm
For thee, my gentle-hearted Charles, to whom
No sound is dissonant which tells of Life.

Teignmouth

John Keats

Here all the summer could I stay,
 For there's Bishop's teign
 And King's teign
And Coomb at the clear teign head –
 Where close by the stream
 You may have your cream
All spread upon barley bread.

There's arch Brook
And there's larch Brook
Both turning many a mill;
And cooling the drouth
Of the salmon's mouth
And fattening his silver gill.

There is Wild wood,
A Mild hood
To the sheep on the lea o' the down,
Where the golden furze,
With its green, thin spurs,
Doth catch at the maiden's gown.

There is Newton marsh
With its spear grass harsh –
A pleasant summer level
Where the maidens sweet
Of the Market Street,
Do meet in the dusk to revel.

There's the Barton rich
With dyke and ditch
And hedge for the thrush to live in
And the hollow tree
For the buzzing bee
And bank for the wasp to hive in.

And O, and O
The daisies blow
And the primroses are awaken
And violets white
Sit in silver plight,
And the green bud's as long as the spike end.

Then who would go
Into dark Soho,
And chatter with dack'd hair'd critics,
When he can stay
For the new-mown hay,
And startle the dappled Prickets?

The White Horse of Westbury

Charles Tennyson Turner

As from the Dorset shore I travelled home,
I saw the charger of the Wiltshire wold;
A far-seen figure, stately to behold,
Whose groom the shepherd is, the hoe his comb;
His wizard-spell even sober daylight owned;
That night I dreamed him into living will;
He neighed – and, straight, the chalk poured down the hill;
He shook himself, and all beneath was stoned;
Hengist and Horsa shouted o'er my sleep,
Like fierce Achilles; while that storm-blanched horse
Sprang to the van of all the Saxon force,
And pushed the Britons to the Western deep;
Then, dream-wise, as it were a thing of course.
He floated upwards, and regained the steep.

Up on the Downs

John Masefield

Up on the downs the red-eyed kestrels hover,
Eyeing the grass.
The field-mouse flits like a shadow into cover
As their shadows pass.

Men are burning the gorse on the down's shoulder;
A drift of smoke
Glitters with fire and hangs, and the skies smoulder,
And the lungs choke.

Once the tribe did thus on the downs, on these downs burning
Men in the frame,
Crying to the gods of the downs till their brains were turning
And the gods came.

And to-day on the downs, in the wind, the hawks, the grasses,
In blood and air,
Something passes me and cries as it passes,
On the chalk downland bare.

Sussex

Rudyard Kipling

God gave all men all earth to love,
  But, since our hearts are small,
Ordained for each one spot should prove
  Belovèd over all;
That, as He watched Creation's birth,
  So we, in godlike mood,
May of our love create our earth
  And see that it is good.

So one shall Baltic pines content,
  As one some Surrey glade,
Or one the palm-grove's droned lament
  Before Levuka's Trade.
Each to his choice, and I rejoice
  The lot has fallen to me
In a fair ground – in a fair ground –
  Yea, Sussex by the sea!

No tender-hearted garden crowns,
  No bosomed woods adorn
Our blunt, bow-headed, whale-backed Downs
  But gnarled and writhen thorn –
Bare slopes where chasing shadows skim,
  And, through the gaps revealed,
Belt upon belt, the wooded, dim,
  Blue goodness of the Weald.

Clean of officious fence or hedge,
  Half-wild and wholly tame,
The wise turf cloaks the white cliff-edge

As when the Romans came.
What sign of those that fought and died
At shift of sword and sword?
The barrow and the camp abide,
The sunlight and the sward.

Here leaps ashore the full Sou'west
All heavy-winged with brine,
Here lies above the folded crest
The Channel's leaden line;
And here the sea-fogs lap and cling,
And here, each warning each,
The sheep bells and the ship-bells ring
Along the hidden beach.

We have no waters to delight
Our broad and brookless vales –
Only the dewpond on the height
Unfed, that never fails –
Whereby no tattered herbage tells
Which way the season flies –
Only our close-bit thyme that smells
Like dawn in Paradise.

Here through the strong and shadeless days
The tinkling silence thrills;
Or little, lost, Down churches praise
The Lord who made the hills:
But here the Old Gods guard their round,
And, in her secret heart,
The heathen kingdom Wilfrid found
Dreams, as she dwells, apart.

Though all the rest were all my share,
With equal soul I'd see
Her nine-and-thirty sisters fair,
Yet none more fair than she.
Choose ye your need from Thames to Tweed,
And I will choose instead
Such lands as lie 'twixt Rake and Rye,
Black Down and Beachy Head.

I will go out against the sun
  Where the rolled scarp retires,
And the Long Man of Wilmington
  Looks naked towards the shires;
And east till doubling Rother crawls
  To find the fickle tide,
By dry and sea-forgotten walls,
  Our ports of stranded pride.

I will go north about the shaws
  And the deep ghylls that breed
Huge oaks and old, the which we hold
  No more than Sussex weed;
Or south where windy Piddinghoe's
  Begilded dolphin veers,
And red beside wide-bankèd Ouse
  Lie down our Sussex steers.

So to the land our hearts we give
  Till the sure magic strike,
And Memory, Use, and Love make live
  Us and our fields alike –
That deeper than our speech and thought,
  Beyond our reason's sway.
Clay of the pit whence we were wrought
  Yearns to its fellow clay.

God gives all men all earth to love,
  But, since man's heart is small,
Ordains for each one spot shall prove
  Belovèd over all.
Each to his choice, and I rejoice
  The lot has fallen to me
In a fair ground – in a fair ground –
  Yea, Sussex by the sea!

Dover Beach

Matthew Arnold

The sea is calm to-night.
The tide is full, the moon lies fair
Upon the straits; – on the French coast the light
Gleams and is gone; the cliffs of England stand,
Glimmering and vast, out in the tranquil bay.
Come to the window, sweet is the night-air!
Only, from the long line of spray
Where the sea meets the moon-blanched land,
Listen! you hear the grating roar
Of pebbles which the waves draw back, and fling,
At their return, up the high strand,
Begin, and cease, and then again begin,
With tremulous cadence slow, and bring
The eternal note of sadness in.

Sophocles long ago
Heard it on the Ægæan, and it brought
Into his mind the turbid ebb and flow
Of human misery; we
Find also in the sound a thought,
Hearing it by this distant northern sea.

The Sea of Faith
Was once, too, at the full, and round earth's shore
Lay like the folds of a bright girdle furled.
But now I only hear
Its melancholy, long, withdrawing roar,
Retreating, to the breath
Of the night-wind, down the vast edges drear
And naked shingles of the world.

Ah, love, let us be true
To one another! for the world, which seems
To lie before us like a land of dreams,
So various, so beautiful, so new,
Hath really neither joy, nor love, nor light,
Nor certitude, nor peace, nor help for pain;
And we are here as on a darkling plain
Swept with confused alarms of struggle and flight,
Where ignorant armies clash by night.

Composed upon Westminster Bridge

William Wordsworth

Earth has not anything to show more fair:
Dull would he be of soul who could pass by
A sight so touching in its majesty:
This City now doth, like a garment, wear
The beauty of the morning; silent, bare,
Ships, towers, domes, theatres, and temples lie
Open unto the fields, and to the sky;
All bright and glittering in the smokeless air.
Never did sun more beautifully steep
In his first splendour, valley, rock, or hill;
Ne'er saw I, never felt, a calm so deep!
The river glideth at his own sweet will:
Dear God! the very houses seem asleep;
And all that mighty heart is lying still!

London Snow

Robert Bridges

When men were all asleep the snow came flying,
In large white flakes falling on the city brown,
Stealthily and perpetually settling and loosely lying,
  Hushing the latest traffic of the drowsy town;
Deadening, muffling, stifling its murmurs failing;
Lazily and incessantly floating down and down:
  Silently sifting and veiling road, roof and railing;
Hiding difference, making unevenness even,
Into angles and crevices softly drifting and sailing.
  All night it fell, and when full inches seven
It lay in the depth of its uncompacted lightness,
The clouds blew off from a high and frosty heaven;
  And all woke earlier for the unaccustomed brightness
Of the winter dawning, the strange unheavenly glare:
The eye marvelled – marvelled at the dazzling whiteness;
  The ear hearkened to the stillness of the solemn air;
No sound of wheel rumbling nor of foot falling,
And the busy morning cries came thin and spare.
  Then boys I heard, as they went to school, calling,
They gathered up the crystal manna to freeze
Their tongues with tasting, their hands with snowballing;
  Or rioted in a drift, plunging up to the knees;
Or peering up from under the white-mossed wonder,
'O look at the trees!' they cried, 'O look at the trees!'
  With lessened load a few carts creak and blunder,
Following along the white deserted way,
A country company long dispersed asunder:
  When now already the sun, in pale display
Standing by Paul's high dome, spread forth below
His sparkling beams, and awoke the stir of the day.
  For now doors open, and war is waged with the snow;
And trains of sombre men, past tale of number,
Tread long brown paths, as toward their toil they go:
  But even for them awhile no cares encumber
Their minds diverted; the daily word is unspoken,
The daily thoughts of labour and sorrow slumber
At the sight of the beauty that greets them, for the charm they have broken.

The Old Vicarage, Grantchester

Rupert Brooke

Just now the lilac is in bloom,
All before my little room;
And in my flower-beds, I think,
Smile the carnation and the pink;
And down the borders, well I know,
The poppy and the pansy blow . . .
Oh! there the chestnuts, summer through,
Beside the river make for you
A tunnel of green gloom, and sleep
Deeply above; and green and deep
The stream mysterious glides beneath,
Green as a dream and deep as death.
– Oh, damn! I know it! and I know
How the May fields all golden show,
And when the day is young and sweet,
Gild gloriously the bare feet
That run to bathe . . .
Du lieber Gott!

Here am I, sweating, sick, and hot,
And there the shadowed waters fresh
Lean up to embrace the naked flesh.

Temperamentvoll German Jews
Drink beer around; – and *there* the dews
Are soft beneath a morn of gold.
Here tulips bloom as they are told;
Unkempt about those hedges blows
An English unofficial rose;
And there the unregulated sun
Slopes down to rest when day is done,
And wages a vague unpunctual star,
A slippered Hesper; and there are
Meads towards Haslingfield and Coton
Where *das Betreten*'s not *verboten*.

εἴθε γενοίμην . . . would I were
In Grantchester, in Grantchester! –
Some, it may be, can get in touch
With Nature there, or Earth, or such.
And clever modern men have seen
A Faun a-peeping through the green,
And felt the Classics were not dead,
To glimpse a Naiad's reedy head,
Or hear the Goat-foot piping low: . . .
But these are things I do not know.
I only know that you may lie
Day-long and watch the Cambridge sky,
And, flower-lulled in sleepy grass,
Hear the cool lapse of hours pass,
Until the centuries blend and blur
In Grantchester, In Grantchester. . . .
Still in the dawnlit waters cool
His ghostly Lordship swims his pool,
And tries the strokes, essays the tricks,
Long learnt on Hellespont, or Styx.
Dan Chaucer hears his river still
Chatter beneath a phantom mill.
Tennyson notes, with studious eye,
How Cambridge waters hurry by . . .
And in that garden, black and white,
Creep whispers through the grass all night;
And spectral dance, before the dawn,
A hundred Vicars down the lawn;

Curates, long dust, will come and go
On lissom, clerical, printless toe;
And oft between the boughs is seen
The sly shade of a Rural Dean . . .
Till, at a shiver in the skies,
Vanishing with Satanic cries,
The prim ecclesiastic rout
Leaves but a startled sleeper-out,
Grey heavens, the first bird's drowsy calls,
The falling house that never falls.

God! I will pack, and take a train,
And get me to England once again!
For England's the one land, I know,
Where men with Splendid Hearts may go;
And Cambridgeshire, of all England,
The shire for Men who Understand;
And of *that* district I prefer
The lovely hamlet Grantchester.
For Cambridge people rarely smile,
Being urban, squat, and packed with guile;
And Royston men in the far South
Are black and fierce and strange of mouth;
At Over they fling oaths at one,
And worse than oaths at Trumpington,
And Ditton girls are mean and dirty,
And there's none in Harston under thirty,
And folks in Shelford and those parts
Have twisted lips and twisted hearts,
And Barton men make Cockney rhymes,
And Coton's full of nameless crimes,
And things are done you'd not believe
At Madingley, on Christmas Eve.
Strong men have run for miles and miles,
When one from Cherry Hinton smiles;
Strong men have blanched, and shot their wives,
Rather than send them to St Ives;
Strong men have cried like babes, bydam,
To hear what happened at Babraham.
But Grantchester! ah, Grantchester!
There's peace and holy quiet there,

Great clouds along pacific skies,
And men and women with straight eyes,
Lithe children lovelier than a dream,
A bosky wood, a slumbrous stream,
And little kindly winds that creep
Round twilight corners, half asleep.
In Grantchester their skins are white;
They bathe by day, they bathe by night;
The women there do all they ought;
The men observe the Rules of Thought.
They love the Good; they worship Truth;
They laugh uproariously in youth;
(And when they get to feeling old,
They up and shoot themselves, I'm told) . . .

Ah God! to see the branches stir
Across the moon at Grantchester!
To smell the thrilling-sweet and rotten
Unforgettable, unforgotten
River-smell, and hear the breeze
Sobbing in the little trees.
Say, do the elm-clumps greatly stand
Still guardians of that holy land?
The chestnuts shade, in reverend dream,
The yet unacademic stream?
Is dawn a secret shy and cold
Anadyomene, silver-gold?
And sunset still a golden sea
From Haslingfield to Madingley?
And after, ere the night is born,
Do hares come out about the corn?
Oh, is the water sweet and cool,
Gentle and brown, above the pool?
And laughs the immortal river still
Under the mill, under the mill?
Say, is there Beauty yet to find?
And Certainty? and Quiet kind?
Deep meadows yet, for to forget
The lies, the truths, and pain? . . . oh! yet
Stands the Church clock at ten to three?
And is there honey still for tea?

Elegy Written in a Country Churchyard

Thomas Gray

The curfew tolls the knell of parting day,
The lowing herd wind slowly o'er the lea,
The ploughman homeward plods his weary way,
And leaves the world to darkness and to me.

Now fades the glimmering landscape on the sight,
And all the air a solemn stillness holds,
Save where the beetle wheels his droning flight,
And drowsy tinklings lull the distant folds;

Save that from yonder ivy-mantled tower
The moping owl does to the moon complain
Of such as, wandering near her secret bower,
Molest her ancient solitary reign.

Beneath those rugged elms, that yew-tree's shade,
Where heaves the turf in many a mouldering heap,
Each in his narrow cell for ever laid,
The rude forefathers of the hamlet sleep.

The breezy call of incense-breathing morn,
The swallow twittering from the straw-built shed,
The cock's shrill clarion or the echoing horn,
No more shall rouse them from their lowly bed.

For them no more the blazing hearth shall burn,
Or busy housewife ply her evening care:
No children run to lisp their sire's return,
Or climb his knees the envied kiss to share.

Oft did the harvest to their sickle yield,
Their furrow oft the stubborn glebe has broke;
How jocund did they drive their team afield!
How bowed the woods beneath their sturdy stroke!

Let not Ambition mock their useful toil,
Their homely joys and destiny obscure;
Nor Grandeur hear, with a disdainful smile,
The short and simple annals of the poor.

The boast of heraldry, the pomp of power,
And all that beauty, all that wealth e'er gave,
Awaits alike the inevitable hour.
The paths of glory lead but to the grave.

Nor you, ye Proud, impute to these the fault,
If Memory ȯ'er their tomb no trophies raise,
Where through the long-drawn aisle and fretted vault
The pealing anthem swells the note of praise.

Can storied urn or animated bust
Back to its mansion call the fleeting breath?
Can Honour's voice provoke the silent dust,
Or Flattery soothe the dull cold ear of Death?

Perhaps in this neglected spot is laid
Some heart once pregnant with celestial fire;
Hands that the rod of empire might have swayed,
Or waked to ecstasy the living lyre.

But Knowledge to their eyes her ample page
Rich with the spoils of time did ne'er unroll;
Chill Penury repressed their noble rage,
And froze the genial current of the soul.

Full many a gem of purest ray serene
The dark unfathomed caves of ocean bear:
Full many a flower is born to blush unseen,
And waste its sweetness on the desert air.

Some village-Hampden that with dauntless breast
The little tyrant of his fields withstood;
Some mute inglorious Milton here may rest,
Some Cromwell guiltless of his country's blood.

The applause of listening senates to command,
The threats of pain and ruin to despise,
To scatter plenty o'er a smiling land,
And read their history in a nation's eyes,

Their lot forbade: nor circumscribed alone
Their growing virtues, but their crimes confined;
Forbade to wade through slaughter to a throne,
And shut the gates of mercy on mankind,

The struggling pangs of conscious truth to hide,
To quench the blushes of ingenuous shame,
Or heap the shrine of Luxury and Pride
With incense kindled at the Muse's flame.

Far from the madding crowd's ignoble strife
Their sober wishes never learned to stray;
Along the cool sequestered vale of life
They kept the noiseless tenor of their way.

Yet even these bones from insult to protect
Some frail memorial still erected nigh,
With uncouth rhymes and shapeless sculpture decked,
Implores the passing tribute of a sigh.

Their name, their years, spelt by the unlettered muse,
The place of fame and elergy supply:
And many a holy text around she strews,
That teach the rustic moralist to die.

For who to dumb Forgetfulness a prey,
This pleasing anxious being e'er resigned,
Left the warm precincts of the cheerful day,
Nor cast one longing lingering look behind?

On some fond breast the parting soul relies,
Some pious drops the closing eye requires;
Even from the tomb the voice of Nature cries,
Even in our ashes live their wonted fires.

For thee who, mindful of the unhonoured dead,
Dost in these lines their artless tale relate;
If chance, by lonely Contemplation led,
Some kindred spirit shall inquire thy fate.

Haply some hoary-headed swain may say,
'Oft have we seen him at the peep of dawn
Brushing with hasty steps the dews away
To meet the sun upon the upland lawn.

'There at the foot of yonder nodding beech
That wreathes its old fantastic roots so high,
His listless length at noontide would he stretch,
And pore upon the brook that babbles by.

'Hard by yon wood, now smiling as in scorn,
Muttering his wayward fancies he would rove,
Now drooping, woeful wan, like one forlorn,
Or crazed with care, or crossed in hopeless love.

'One morn I missed him on the customed hill,
Along the heath and near his favourite tree;
Another came; nor yet beside the rill,
Nor up the lawn, nor at the wood was he;

'The next with dirges due in sad array
Slow through the church-way path we saw him borne.
Approach and read (for thou canst read) the lay,
Graved on the stone beneath yon aged thorn.'

The Epitaph

Here rests his head upon the lap of earth
A youth to Fortune and to Fame unknown.
Fair Science frowned not on his humble birth,
And Melancholy marked him for her own.

Large was his bounty and his soul sincere,
Heaven did a recompense as largely send:
He gave to Misery all he had, a tear,
He gained from Heaven ('twas all he wished) a friend.

No farther seek his merits to disclose,
Or draw his frailties from their dread abode,
(There they alike in trembling hope repose)
The bosom of his Father and his God.

ADLESTROP

Edward Thomas

Yes. I remember Adlestrop –
The name, because one afternoon
Of heat the express-train drew up there
Unwontedly. It was late June.

The steam hissed. Someone cleared his throat
No one left and no one came
On the bare platform. What I saw
Was Adlestrop – only the name

And willows, willow-herb, and grass,
And meadowsweet, and haycocks dry,
No whit less still and lonely fair
Than the high cloudlets in the sky.

And for that minute a blackbird sang
Close by, and round him, mistier,
Farther and farther, all the birds
Of Oxfordshire and Gloucestershire.

from

Lines Composed a few Miles Above Tintern Abbey

William Wordsworth

Five years have past; five summers, with the length
Of five long winters! and again I hear
These waters, rolling from their mountain-springs
With a soft inland murmur. – Once again
Do I behold these steep and lofty cliffs,
That on a wild secluded scene impress
Thoughts of more deep seclusion; and connect
The landscape with the quiet of the sky.
The day is come when I again repose
Here, under this dark sycamore, and view
These plots of cottage-ground, these orchard-tufts,
Which at this season, with their unripe fruits,
Are clad in one green hue, and lose themselves
'Mid groves and copses. Once again I see
These hedge-rows, hardly hedge-rows, little lines
Of sportive wood run wild: these pastoral farms,
Green to the very door; and wreaths of smoke
Sent up, in silence, from among the trees!
With some uncertain notice, as might seem
Of vagrant dwellers in the houseless woods,
Or of some Hermit's cave, where by his fire
The Hermit sits alone.

These beauteous forms,
Through a long absence, have not been to me
As is a landscape to a blind man's eye:
But oft, in lonely rooms, and 'mid the din
Of towns and cities, I have owed to them
In hours of weariness, sensations sweet,
Felt in the blood, and felt along the heart;
And passing even into my purer mind,
With tranquil restoration: – feelings too
Of unremembered pleasure: such, perhaps,
As have no slight or trivial influence

On that best portion of a good man's life,
His little, nameless, unremembered, acts
Of kindness and of love. Nor less, I trust,
To them I may have owed another gift,
Of aspect more sublime; that blessed mood,
In which the burthen of the mystery,
In which the heavy and the weary weight
Of all this unintelligible world
Is lightened: – that serene and blessed mood,
In which the affections gently lead us on, –
Until, the breath of this corporeal frame
And even the motion of our human blood
Almost suspended, we are laid asleep
In body, and become a living soul:
While with an eye made quiet by the power
Of harmony, and the deep power of joy,
We see into the life of things.

If this
Be but a vain belief, yet, oh! how oft –
In darkness and amid the many shapes
Of joyless daylight; when the fretful stir
Unprofitable, and the fever of the world,
Have hung upon the beatings of my heart –
How oft, in spirit, have I turned to thee,
O sylvan Wye! thou wanderer thro' the woods,
How often has my spirit turned to thee!
And now, with gleams of half-extinguished thought,
With many recognitions dim and faint,
And somewhat of a sad perplexity,
The picture of the mind revives again:
While here I stand, not only with the sense
Of present pleasure, but with pleasing thoughts
That in this moment there is life and food
For future years. And so I dare to hope,
Though changed, no doubt, from what I was when first
I came among these hills; when like a roe
I bounded o'er the mountains, by the sides
Of the deep rivers, and the lonely streams,
Wherever nature led: more like a man

Flying from something that he dreads, than one
Who sought the thing he loved. For nature then
(The coarser pleasures of my boyish days,
And their glad animal movements all gone by)
To me was all in all. – I cannot paint
What then I was. The sounding cataract
Haunted me like a passion: the tall rock,
The mountain, and the deep and gloomy wood,
Their colours and their forms, were then to me
An appetite; a feeling and a love,
That had no need of a remoter charm,
By thought supplied, nor any interest
Unborrowed from the eye. – That time is past,
And all its aching joys are now no more,
And all its dizzy raptures. Not for this
Faint I, nor mourn nor murmur; other gifts
Have followed; for such loss, I would believe,
Abundant recompence. For I have learned
To look on nature, not as in the hour
Of thoughtless youth; but hearing oftentimes
The still, sad music of humanity,
Nor harsh nor grating, though of ample power
To chasten and subdue. And I have felt
A presence that disturbs me with the joy
Of elevated thoughts; a sense sublime
Of something far more deeply interfused,
Whose dwelling is the light of setting suns,
And the round ocean and the living air,
And the blue sky, and in the mind of man:
A motion and a spirit, that impels
All thinking things, all objects of all thought,
And rolls through all things. Therefore am I still
A lover of the meadows and the woods,
And mountains; and of all that we behold
From this green earth; of all the mighty world
Of eye, and ear, – both what they half create,
And what perceive; well pleased to recognise
In nature and the language of the sense,
The anchor of my purest thoughts, the nurse,
The guide, the guardian of my heart, and soul
Of all my moral being.

Fern Hill

Dylan Thomas

Now as I was young and easy under the apple boughs
About the lilting house and happy as the grass was green,
   The night above the dingle starry,
      Time let me hail and climb
   Golden in the heydays of his eyes,
And honoured among wagons I was prince of the apple towns
And once below a time I lordly had the trees and leaves
      Trail with daisies and barley
   Down the rivers of the windfall light.

And as I was green and carefree, famous among the barns
About the happy yard and singing as the farm was home,
   In the sun that is young once only,
      Time let me play and be
   Golden in the mercy of his means,
And green and golden I was huntsman and herdsman, the calves
Sang to my horn, the foxes on the hills barked clear and cold.
      And the sabbath rang slowly
   In the pebbles of the holy streams.

All the sun long it was running, it was lovely, the hay
Fields high as the house, the tunes from the chimneys, it was air
    And playing, lovely and watery
        And fire green as grass.
    And nightly under the simple stars
As I rode to sleep the owls were bearing the farm away,
All the moon long I heard, blessed among stables, the night-jars
    Flying with the ricks, and the horses
        Flashing into the dark.

And then to awake, and the farm, like a wanderer white
With the dew, come back, the cock on his shoulder: it was all
    Shining, it was Adam and maiden,
        The sky gathered again
    And the sun grew round that very day.
So it must have been after the birth of the simple light
In the first, spinning place, the spellbound horses walking warm
    Out of the whinnying green stable
        On to the fields of praise.

And honoured among foxes and pheasants by the gay house
Under the new made clouds and happy as the heart was long,
    In the sun born over and over,
        I ran my heedless ways,
    My wishes raced through the house high hay
And nothing I cared, at my sky blue trades, that time allows
In all his tuneful turning so few and such morning songs
    Before the children green and golden
        Follow him out of grace,

Nothing I cared, in the lamb white days, that time would take me
Up to the swallow thronged loft by the shadow of my hand,
    In the moon that is always rising,
        Nor that riding to sleep
    I should hear him fly with the high fields
And wake to the farm forever fled from the childless land.
Oh as I was young and easy in the mercy of his means,
        Time held me green and dying
Though I sang in my chains like the sea.

The Welsh Hill Country

R.S. Thomas

Too far for you to see
The fluke and the foot-rot and the fat maggot
Gnawing the skin from the small bones,
The sheep are grazing at Bwlch-y-Fedwen,
Arranged romantically in the usual manner
On a bleak background of bald stone.

Too far for you to see
The moss and the mould on the cold chimneys,
The nettles growing through the cracked doors,
The houses stand empty at Nant-yr-Eira,
There are holes in the roofs that are thatched with sunlight,
And the fields are reverting to the bare moor.

Too far, too far to see
The set of his eyes and the slow phthisis
Wasting his frame under the ripped coat,
There's a man still farming at Ty'n-y-Fawnog,
Contributing grimly to the accepted pattern,
The embryo music dead in his throat.

Pennines in April

Ted Hughes

If this country were a sea (that is solid rock
Deeper than any sea) these hills heaving
Out of the east, mass behind mass, at this height
Hoisting heather and stones to the sky
Must burst upwards and topple into Lancashire.

Perhaps, as the earth turns, such ground-stresses
Do come rolling westward through the locked land.
Now, measuring the miles of silence
Your eye takes the strain: through

Landscapes gliding blue as water
Those barrellings of strength are heaving slowly and heave
To your feet and surf upwards
In a still, fiery air, hauling the imagination,
Carrying the larks upward.

Winter in the Fens

John Clare

So moping flat and low our valleys lie,
So dull and muggy is our winter sky,
Drizzling from day to day with threats of rain,
And when that falls still threatening on again;
From one wet week so great an ocean flows
That every village to an island grows,
And every road for even weeks to come
Is stopt, and none but horsemen go from home;
And one wet night leaves travel's best in doubt,
And horseback travellers ask if floods are out
Of every passer-by, and with their horse
The meadow's ocean try in vain to cross;
The horse's footings with a sucking sound
Fill up with water on the firmest ground,
And ruts that dribble into brooks elsewhere
Can find no fall or flat to dribble here,
But filled with wet they brim and overflow
Till hollows in the road to rivers grow;
Then wind with sudden rage, abrupt and blea,
Twirls every lingering leaf from off each tree.
Such is our lowland scene that winter gives,
And strangers wonder where our comfort lives;
Yet in a little close, however keen
The winter comes, I find a patch of green,
Where robins, by the miser winter made
Domestic, flirt and perch upon the spade;
And in a little garden-close at home
I watch for spring – and there's the crocus come!

AMID THE BARREN HILLS

Emily Brontë

There is a spot, 'mid barren hills,
  Where winter howls, and driving rain;
But, if the dreary tempest chills,
  There is a light that warms again.

The house is old, the trees are bare,
  Moonless above bends twilight's dome;
But what on earth is half so dear –
  So longed for – as the hearth of home?

The mute bird sitting on the stone,
  The dank moss dripping from the wall,
The thorn-trees gaunt, the walks o'ergrown,
  I love them – how I love them all! . . .

A little and a lone green lane
  That opened on a common wide;
A distant, dreamy, dim blue chain
  Of mountains, circling every side.

A heaven so clear, an earth so calm,
  So sweet, so soft, so hushed an air;
And, deepening still the dream-like charm,
  Wild moor-sheep feeding everywhere.

I Wandered Lonely as a Cloud

William Wordsworth

I wandered lonely as a cloud
That floats on high o'er vales and hills,
When all at once I saw a crowd,
A host, of golden daffodils;
Beside the lake, beneath the trees,
Fluttering and dancing in the breeze.

Continuous as the stars that shine
And twinkle on the milky way,
They stretched in never-ending line
Along the margin of a bay:
Ten thousand saw I at a glance,
Tossing their heads in sprightly dance.

The waves beside them danced; but they
Out-did the sparkling waves in glee:
A poet could not but be gay,
In such a jocund company:
I gazed – and gazed – but little thought
What wealth the show to me had brought:

For oft, when on my couch I lie
In vacant or in pensive mood,
They flash upon that inward eye
Which is the bliss of solitude;
And then my heart with pleasure fills,
And dances with the daffodils.

from THE PRELUDE

William Wordsworth

Fair seed-time had my soul, and I grew up
Foster'd alike by beauty and by fear;
Much favor'd in my birthplace, and no less
In that beloved Vale to which, erelong,
I was transplanted. Well I call to mind
('Twas at an early age, ere I had seen
Nine summers) when upon the mountain slope
The frost and breath of frosty wind had snapp'd
The last autumnal crocus, 'twas my joy
To wander half the night among the Cliffs
And the smooth Hollows, where the woodcocks ran
Along the open turf. In thought and wish
That time, my shoulder all with springes hung,
I was a fell destroyer. On the heights
Scudding away from snare to snare, I plied
My anxious visitation, hurrying on,
Still hurrying, hurrying onward; moon and stars

Were shining o'er my head; I was alone,
And seem'd to be a trouble to the peace
That was among them. Sometimes it befel
In these night-wanderings, that a strong desire
O'erpower'd my better reason, and the bird
Which was the captive of another's toils
Became my prey; and, when the deed was done
I heard among the solitary hills
Low breathings coming after me, and sounds
Of undistinguishable motion, steps
Almost as silent as the turf they trod.
Nor less in springtime when on southern banks
The shining sun had from his knot of leaves
Decoy'd the primrose flower, and when the Vales
And woods were warm, was I a plunderer then
In the high places, on the lonesome peaks
Where'er, among the mountains and the winds,
The Mother Bird had built her lodge. Though mean
My object, and inglorious, yet the end
Was not ignoble. Oh! when I have hung
Above the raven's nest, by knots of grass
And half-inch fissures in the slippery rock
But ill sustain'd, and almost, as it seem'd,
Suspended by the blast which blew amain,
Shouldering the naked crag; Oh! at that time,
While on the perilous ridge I hung alone,
With what strange utterance did the loud dry wind
Blow through my ears! the sky seem'd not a sky
Of earth, and with what motion mov'd the clouds!

The mind of Man is fram'd even like the breath
And harmony of music. There is a dark
Invisible workmanship that reconciles
Discordant elements, and makes them move
In one society. Ah me! that all
The terrors, all the early miseries
Regrets, vexations, lassitudes, that all
The thoughts and feelings which have been infus'd
Into my mind, should ever have made up
The calm existence that is mine when I
Am worthy of myself! Praise to the end!

Thanks likewise for the means! But I believe
That Nature, oftentimes, when she would frame
A favor'd Being, from his earliest dawn
Of infancy doth open out the clouds,
As at the touch of lightning, seeking him
With gentlest visitation; not the less,
Though haply aiming at the self-same end,
Does it delight her sometimes to employ
Severer interventions, ministry
More palpable, and so she dealt with me.

One evening (surely I was led by her)
I went alone into a Shepherd's Boat,
A Skiff that to a Willow tree was tied
Within a rocky Cave, its usual home.
'Twas by the shores of Patterdale, a Vale
Wherein I was a Stranger, thither come
A School-boy Traveller, at the Holidays.
Forth rambled from the Village Inn alone
No sooner had I sight of this small Skiff,
Discover'd thus by unexpected chance,
Than I unloos'd her tether and embark'd.
The moon was up, the Lake was shining clear
Among the hoary mountains; from the Shore
I push'd, and struck the oars and struck again
In cadence, and my little Boat mov'd on
Even like a Man who walks with stately step
Though bent on speed. It was an act of stealth
And troubled pleasure; not without the voice
Of mountain-echoes did my Boat move on,
Leaving behind her still on either side
Small circles glittering idly in the moon,
Until they melted all into one track
Of sparkling light. A rocky Steep uprose
Above the Cavern of the Willow tree
And now, as suited one who proudly row'd
With his best skill, I fix'd a steady view
Upon the top of that same craggy ridge,
The bound of the horizon, for behind
Was nothing but the stars and the grey sky.
She was an elfin Pinnace; lustily

I dipp'd my oars into the silent Lake,
And, as I rose upon the stroke, my Boat
Went heaving through the water, like a Swan;
When from behind that craggy Steep, till then
The bound of the horizon, a huge Cliff,
As if with voluntary power instinct,
Uprear'd its head. I struck, and struck again,
And, growing still in stature, the huge Cliff
Rose up between me and the stars, and still,
With measur'd motion, like a living thing,
Strode after me. With trembling hands I turn'd,
And through the silent water stole my way
Back to the Cavern of the Willow tree.
There, in her mooring-place, I left my Bark,
And, through the meadows homeward went, with grave
And serious thoughts; and after I had seen
That spectacle, for many days, my brain
Work'd with a dim and undetermin'd sense
Of unknown modes of being; in my thoughts
There was a darkness, call it solitude,
Or blank desertion, no familiar shapes
Of hourly objects, images of trees,
Of sea or sky, no colours of green fields;
But huge and mighty Forms that do not live
Like living men mov'd slowly through my mind
By day and were the trouble of my dreams.

Wisdom and Spirit of the universe!
Thou Soul that art the Eternity of Thought!
That giv'st to forms and images a breath
And everlasting motion! not in vain,
By day or star-light thus from my first dawn
Of Childhood didst Thou intertwine for me
The passions that build up our human Soul,
Not with the mean and vulgar works of Man,
But with high objects, with enduring things,
With life and nature, purifying thus
The elements of feeling and of thought,
And sanctifying, by such discipline
Both pain and fear, until we recognize
A grandeur in the beatings of the heart.

O Caledonia!

Sir Walter Scott

O Caledonia! stern and wild,
Meet nurse for a poetic child!
Land of brown heath and shaggy wood,
Land of the mountain and the flood,
Land of my sires! what mortal hand
Can e'er untie the filial band,
That knits me to thy rugged strand!
Still, as I view each well known scene,
Think what is now, and what hath been,
Seems as, to me, of all bereft,
Sole friends thy woods and streams were left;
And thus I love them better still,
Even in extremity of ill.

By Yarrow's stream still let me stray,
Though none should guide my feeble way;
Still feel the breeze down Ettricke break,
Although it chill my withered cheek;
Still lay my head by Teviot Stone,
Though there, forgotten and alone,
The Bard may draw his parting groan.

Scotland Small?

Hugh MacDiarmid

Scotland small? Our multiform, our infinite Scotland *small*?
Only as a patch of hillside may be a cliché corner
To a fool who cries 'Nothing but heather!' Where in September another
Sitting there and resting and gazing round
Sees not only heather but blaeberries
With bright green leaves and leaves already turned scarlet,
Hiding ripe blue berries; and amongst the sage-green leaves
Of the bog-myrtle the golden flowers of the tormentil shining;
And on the small bare places, where the little Blackface sheep
Found grazing, milkworts blue as summer skies;
And down in neglected peat-hags, not worked
In living memory, sphagnum moss in pastel shades
Of yellow, green, and pink; sundew and butterwort
And nodding harebells vying in their colour
With the blue butterflies that poise themselves delicately upon them.
And stunted rowans with harsh dry leaves of glorious colour
'Nothing but heather!' – How marvellously descriptive! And incomplete!

My Heart's in the Highlands

Robert Burns

My heart's in the Highlands, my heart is not here;
My heart's in the Highlands a chasing the deer;
Chasing the wild deer, and following the roe;
My heart's in the Highlands, wherever I go. –

Farewell to the Highlands, farewell to the North;
The birth-place of valour, the country of worth:
Wherever I wander, wherever I rove,
The hills of the Highlands for ever I love. –

Farewell to the mountains high cover'd with snow;
Farewell to the Straths and green valleys below:
Farewell to the forests and wild-hanging woods;
Farewell to the torrents and loud-pouring floods. –

My heart's in the Highlands, my heart is not here;
My heart's in the Highlands a chasing the deer;
Chasing the wild deer, and following the roe;
My heart's in the Highlands, wherever I go. –

Inversnaid

Gerard Manley Hopkins

This darksome burn, horseback brown,
His rollrock highroad roaring down,
In coop and in comb the fleece of his foam
Flutes and low to the lake falls home.

A windpuff-bonnet of fáwn-fróth
Turns and twindles over the broth
Of a pool so pitchblack, féll frówning,
It rounds and rounds Despair to drowning.

Degged with dew, dappled with dew
Are the groins of the braes that the brook treads through,
Wiry heathpacks, flitches of fern,
And the beadbonny ash that sits over the burn.

What would the world be, once bereft
Of wet and of wildness? Let them be left,
O let them be left, wildness and wet;
Long live the weeds and the wilderness yet.

PART THREE

'A Bold Peasantry'

'Ill fares the land, to hastening ills a prey,
Where wealth accumulates and men decay:
Princes and lords may flourish or may fade;
A breath can make them, as a breath has made;
But a bold peasantry, their country's pride,
When once destroyed can never be supplied.'

from The Deserted Village

Oliver Goldsmith

Sweet smiling village, loveliest of the lawn,
Thy sports are fled and all thy charms withdrawn;
Amidst thy bowers the tyrant's hand is seen,
And desolation saddens all thy green;
One only master grasps the whole domain,
And half a tillage stints thy smiling plain;
No more thy glassy brook reflects the day,
But, choked with sedges, works its weedy way;
Along thy glades, a solitary guest,
The hollow-sounding bittern guards its nest;
Amidst thy desert walks the lapwing flies,
And tires their echoes with unvaried cries;
Sunk are thy bowers in shapeless ruin all,
And the long grass o'ertops the mouldering wall;
And trembling, shrinking from the spoiler's hand,
Far, far away, thy children leave the land.
  Ill fares the land, to hastening ills a prey,
Where wealth accumulates and men decay:
Princes and lords may flourish or may fade;
A breath can make them, as a breath has made;
But a bold peasantry, their country's pride,
When once destroyed, can never be supplied.
  A time there was, ere England's griefs began,
When every rood of ground maintained its man;
For him light labour spread her wholesome store,
Just gave what life required, but gave no more:
His best companions, innocence and health;
And his best riches, ignorance of wealth.
  But times are altered; trade's unfeeling train
Usurp the land and dispossess the swain;
Along the lawn, where scattered hamlets rose,

Unwieldy wealth and cumbrous pomp repose;
And every want to opulence allied,
And every pang that folly pays to pride.
Those gentle hours that plenty bade to bloom,
Those calm desires that asked but little room,
Those healthful sports that graced the peaceful scene,
Lived in each look and brightened all the green;
These, far departing, seek a kinder shore,
And rural mirth and manners are no more.
   Sweet Auburn! parent of the blissful hour,
Thy glades forlorn confess the tyrant's power.
Here as I take my solitary rounds,
Amidst thy tangling walks and ruined grounds,
And, many a year elapsed, return to view
Where once the cottage stood, the hawthorn grew,
Remembrance wakes with all her busy train,
Swells at my breast, and turns the past to pain.
   In all my wanderings round this world of care,
In all my griefs – and God has given my share –
I still had hopes my latest hours to crown,
Amidst these humble bowers to lay me down;
To husband out life's taper at the close,
And keep the flame from wasting by repose.
I still had hopes, for pride attends us still,
Amidst the swains to show my book-learned skill,
Around my fire an evening group to draw,
And tell of all I felt and all I saw;
And, as a hare whom hounds and horns pursue
Pants to the place from whence at first she flew,
I still had hopes, my long vexations past,
Here to return – and die at home at last.
   O blest retirement, friend to life's decline,
Retreats from care, that never must be mine,
How happy he who crowns in shades like these
A youth of labour with an age of ease;
Who quits a world where strong temptations try
And, since 'tis hard to combat, learns to fly!
For him no wretches, born to work and weep,
Explore the mine or tempt the dangerous deep;
No surly porter stands in guilty state
To spurn imploring famine from the gate;

But on he moves to meet his latter end,
Angels around befriending virtue's friend;
Bends to the grave with unperceived decay,
While resignation gently slopes the way;
And, all his prospects brightening to the last,
His heaven commences ere the world be past!
Sweet was the sound, when oft at evening's close
Up yonder hill the village murmur rose;
There, as I passed with careless steps and slow,
The mingling notes came softened from below;
The swain responsive as the milkmaid sung,
The sober herd that lowed to meet their young;
The noisy geese that gabbled o'er the pool,
The playful children just let loose from school;
The watchdog's voice that bayed the whispering wind,
And the loud laugh that spoke the vacant mind;
These all in sweet confusion sought the shade,
And filled each pause the nightingale had made.
But now the sounds of population fail,
No cheerful murmurs fluctuate in the gale,
No busy steps the grass-grown foot-way tread,
For all the bloomy flush of life is fled.
All but yon widowed, solitary thing
That feebly bends beside the plashy spring;
She, wretched matron, forced, in age, for bread,
To strip the brook with mantling cresses spread,
To pick her wintry faggot from the thorn,
To seek her nightly shed and weep till morn;
She only left of all the harmless train,
The sad historian of the pensive plain.
Near yonder copse, when once the garden smiled,
And still where many a garden flower grows wild;
There, where a few torn shrubs the place disclose,
The village preacher's modest mansion rose.
A man he was to all the country dear,
And passing rich with forty pounds a year;
Remote from towns he ran his godly race,
Nor e'er had changed, nor wished to change, his place;
Unpractised he to fawn, or seek for power,
By doctrines fashioned to the varying hour;
Far other aims his heart had learned to prize,

More skilled to raise the wretched than to rise.
His house was known to all the vagrant train,
He chid their wanderings, but relieved their pain;
The long-remembered beggar was his guest,
Whose beard descending swept his agèd breast;
The ruined spendthrift, now no longer proud,
Claimed kindred there and had his claims allowed;
The broken soldier, kindly bade to stay,
Sat by his fire and talked the night away;
Wept o'er his wounds, or tales of sorrow done,
Shouldered his crutch, and showed how fields were won.
Pleased with his guests, the good man learned to glow,
And quite forgot their vices in their woe;
Careless their merits or their faults to scan,
His pity gave ere charity began.
  Thus to relieve the wretched was his pride,
And even his failings leaned to virtue's side;
But in his duty prompt at every call,
He watched and wept, he prayed and felt, for all.
And, as a bird each fond endearment tries
To tempt its new-fledged offspring to the skies,
He tried each art, reproved each dull delay,
Allured to brighter worlds and led the way.
  Beside thc bed where parting life was laid,
And sorrow, guilt and pain by turns dismayed,
The reverend champion stood. At his control,
Despair and anguish fled the struggling soul;
Comfort came down the trembling wretch to raise,
And his last faltering accents whispered praise.
  At church, with meek and unaffected grace,
His looks adorned the venerable place;
Truth from his lips prevailed with double sway,
And fools, who came to scoff, remained to pray.
The service past, around the pious man,
With steady zeal, each honest rustic ran;
Even children followed with endearing wile,
And plucked his gown, to share the good man's smile.
His ready smile a parent's warmth expressed,
Their welfare pleased him and their cares distressed;
To them his heart, his love, his griefs were given,
But all his serious thoughts had rest in Heaven.

As some tall cliff that lifts its awful form,
Swells from the vale, and midway leaves the storm,
Though round its breast the rolling clouds are spread,
Eternal sunshine settles on its head.
   Beside yon straggling fence that skirts the way,
With blossomed furze unprofitably gay,
There, in his noisy mansion, skilled to rule,
The village master taught his little school;
A man severe he was, and stern to view;
I knew him well, and every truant knew;
Well had the boding tremblers learned to trace
The day's disasters in his morning face;
Full well they laughed, with counterfeited glee,
At all his jokes, for many a joke had he;
Full well the busy whisper, circling round,
Conveyed the dismal tidings when he frowned;
Yet he was kind, or, if severe in aught,
The love he bore to learning was in fault;
The village all declared how much he knew;
'Twas certain he could write and cipher too;
Lands he could measure, terms and tides presage,
And even the story ran that he could gauge.
In arguing too, the parson owned his skill,
For even though vanquished, he could argue still;
While words of learnèd length and thundering sound
Amazed the gazing rustics ranged around,
And still they gazed, and still the wonder grew,
That one small head could carry all he knew.
   But past is all his fame. The very spot
Where many a time he triumphed is forgot.
Near yonder thorn, that lifts its head on high,
Where once the signpost caught the passing eye,
Low lies that house where nutbrown draughts inspired,
Where greybeard mirth and smiling toil retired,
Where village statesmen talked with looks profound,
And news much older than their ale went round.
Imagination fondly stoops to trace
The parlour splendours of that festive place;
The white-washed wall, the nicely sanded floor,
The varnished clock that clicked behind the door;
The chest contrived a double debt to pay,

A bed by night, a chest of drawers by day;
The pictures placed for ornament and use,
The twelve good rules, the royal game of goose;
The hearth, except when winter chilled the day,
With aspen boughs and flowers and fennel gay;
While broken tea-cups, wisely kept for show,
Ranged o'er the chimney, glistened in a row.
   Vain, transitory splendours! Could not all
Reprieve the tottering mansion from its fall!
Obscure it sinks, nor shall it more impart
An hour's importance to the poor man's heart;
Thither no more the peasant shall repair
To sweet oblivion of his daily care;
No more the farmer's news, the barber's tale,
No more the woodman's ballad shall prevail;
No more the smith his dusky brow shall clear,
Relax his ponderous strength and lean to hear;
The host himself no longer shall be found
Careful to see the mantling bliss go round;
Nor the coy maid, half willing to be pressed,
Shall kiss the cup to pass it to the rest.
   Yes! let the rich deride, the proud disdain,
These simple blessings of the lowly train;
To me more dear, congenial to my heart,
One native charm than all the gloss of art;
Spontaneous joys, where Nature has its play,
The soul adopts and owns their first-born sway;
Lightly they frolic o'er the vacant mind,
Unenvied, unmolested, unconfined.
But the long pomp, the midnight masquerade,
With all the freaks of wanton wealth arrayed,
In these, ere triflers half their wish obtain,
The toiling pleasure sickens into pain;
And, e'en while fashion's brightest arts decoy,
The heart distrusting asks if this be joy.
   Ye friends to truth, ye statesmen, who survey
The rich man's joys increase, the poor's decay,
'Tis yours to judge how wide the limits stand
Between a splendid and a happy land.

The Reaper

William Wordsworth

Behold her, single in the field,
Yon solitary Highland Lass!
Reaping and singing by herself;
Stop here, or gently pass!
Alone she cuts and binds the grain,
And sings a melancholy strain;
O listen! for the vale profound
Is overflowing with the sound.

No nightingale did ever chaunt
More welcome notes to weary bands
Of travellers in some shady haunt,
Among Arabian sands:
No sweeter voice was ever heard
In spring-time from the cuckoo-bird,
Breaking the silence of the seas
Among the farthest Hebrides.

Will no one tell me what she sings?
Perhaps the plaintive numbers flow
For old, unhappy, far-off things,
And battles long ago:
Or is it some more humble lay,
Familiar matter of to-day?
Some natural sorrow, loss, or pain,
That has been, and may be again!

Whate'er the theme, the maiden sang
As if her song could have no ending;
I saw her singing at her work,
And o'er the sickle bending;
I listen'd, till I had my fill;
And, as I mounted up the hill,
The music in my heart I bore
Long after it was heard no more.

The Old Workman

Thomas Hardy

'Why are you so bent down before your time,
Old mason? Many have not left their prime
So far behind at your age, and can still
  Stand full upright at will.'

He pointed to the mansion-front hard by,
And to the stones of the quoin against the sky;
'Those upper blocks,' he said, 'that there you see,
  It was that ruined me.'

There stood in the air up to the parapet
Crowning the corner height, the stones as set
By him – ashlar whereon the gales might drum
  For centuries to come.

'I carried them up,' he said, 'by a ladder there;
The last was as big a load as I could bear;
But on I heaved; and something in my back
  Moved, as 'twere with a crack.

'So I got crookt. I never lost that sprain;
And those who live there, walled from wind and rain
By freestone that I lifted, do not know
  That my life's ache came so.

'They don't know me, or even know my name,
But good I think it, somehow, all the same
To have kept 'em safe from harm, and right and tight,
  Though it has broke me quite.

'Yes; that I fixed it firm up there I am proud,
Facing the hail and snow and sun and cloud,
And to stand storms for ages, beating round
  When I lie underground.'

The Waggon-maker

John Masefield

I have made tales in verse, but this man made
Waggons of elm to last a hundred years;
The blacksmith forged the rims and iron gears,
His was the magic that the wood obeyed.

Each deft device that country wisdom bade,
Or farmers' practice needed, he preserved.
He wrought the subtle contours, straight and curved,
Only by eye, and instinct of the trade.

No weakness, no offence in any part,
It stood the strain in mired fields and roads
In all a century's struggle for its bread;
Bearing, perhaps, eight thousand heavy loads.
Beautiful always as a work of art,
Homing the bride, and harvest, and men dead.

Under the Woods

Edward Thomas

When these old woods were young
The thrushes' ancestors
As sweetly sung
In the old years.

There was no garden here,
Apples nor mistletoe;
No children dear
Ran to and fro.

New then was this thatched cot,
But the keeper was old,
And he had not
Much lead or gold.

Most silent beech and yew:
As he went round about
The woods to view
Seldom he shot.

But now that he is gone
Out of most memories;
Still lingers on,
A stoat of his,

But one, shrivelled and green,
And with no scent at all,
And barely seen
On this shed wall.

Mole Catcher

Edmund Blunden

With coat like any mole's, as soft and black,
And hazel bows bundled beneath his arm,
With long-helved spade and rush bag on his back,
The trapper plods alone about the farm:
And spies new mounds in the ripe pasture-land,
And where the lob-worms writhe up in alarm
And easy sinks the spade, he takes his stand
Knowing the moles' dark highroad runs below:
Then sharp and square he chops the turf, and day
Gloats on the opened turnpike through the clay.

Out from his wallet hurry pin and prong,
And trap, and noose to tie it to the brow;
And then his grand arcanum, oily and strong,
Found out by his forefather years ago
To scent the peg and witch the moles along.
The bow is earthed and arched ready to shoot
And snatch the death-knot fast round the first mole
Who comes and snuffs well pleased and tries to root
Past the sly nose peg; back again is put
The mould, and death left smirking in the hole.
The old man goes and tallies all his snares
And finds the prisoners there and takes his toll.

And moles to him are only moles; but hares
See him afield and scarcely cease to nip
Their dinners, for he harms not them; he spares
The drowning fly that of his ale would sip
And throws the ant the crumbs of comradeship.
And every time he comes into his yard
Grey linnet knows he brings the groundsel sheaf,
And clatters round the cage to be unbarred,
And on his finger whistles twice as hard. –
What his old vicar says, is his belief,
In the side pew he sits and hears the truth;
And never misses once to ring his bell
On Sundays night and more, nor once since youth
Has heard the chimes afield, but has heard tell
There's not a peal in England sounds so well.

The Old Squire

Wilfred Scawen Blunt

I like the hunting of the hare
Better than that of the fox;
I like the joyous morning air,
And the crowing of the cocks.

I like the calm of the early fields,
The ducks asleep by the lake,
The quiet hour which Nature yields,
Before mankind is awake.

I like the pheasants and feeding things
Of the unsuspicious morn;
I like the flap of the wood-pigeon's wings
As she rises from the corn.

I like the blackbird's shriek, and his rush
From the turnips as I pass by,
And the partridge hiding her head in a bush
For her young ones cannot fly.

I like these things and I like to ride
When all the world is in bed,
To the top of the hill where the sky grows wide,
And where the sun grows red.

The beagles at my horse heels trot
In silence after me;
There's Ruby, Roger, Diamond, Dot,
Old Slut and Margery, –

A score of names well used, and dear,
The names my childhood knew;
The horn, with which I rouse their cheer,
Is the horn my father blew.

I like the hunting of the hare
  Better than that of the fox;
The new world still is all less fair
  Than the old world it mocks.

I covet not a wider range
  Than those dear manors give;
I take my pleasures without change,
  And as I lived I live.

I leave my neighbours to their thought;
My choice it is, and pride,
On my own lands to find my sport,
In my own fields to ride.

The hare herself no better loves
The field where she was bred,
Than I the habit of these groves,
My own inherited.

I know my quarries every one,
The meuse where she sits low;
The road she chose to-day was run
A hundred years ago.

The lags, the gills, the forest ways,
The hedgerows one and all,
These are the kingdoms of my chase,
And bounded by my wall;

Nor has the world a better thing,
Though one should search it round,
Than thus to live one's own sole king,
Upon one's own sole ground.

I like the hunting of the hare;
It brings me, day by day,
The memory of old days as fair,
With dead men past away.

To these, as homeward still I ply
And pass the churchyard gate
Where all are laid as I must lie,
I stop and raise my hat.

I like the hunting of the hare;
New sports I hold in scorn.
I like to be as my fathers were,
In the days e'er I was born.

Meg Merrilees

John Keats

Old Meg she was a Gipsy,
  And lived upon the moors:
Her bed it was the brown heath turf,
  And her house was out of doors.

Her apples were swart blackberries,
  Her currants pods o' broom;
Her wine was dew of the wild white rose,
  Her book a churchyard tomb.

Her Brothers were the craggy hills,
  Her Sisters larchen trees;
Alone with her great family
  She lived as she did please.

No breakfast had she many a morn,
  No dinner many a noon,
And 'stead of supper she would stare
  Full hard against the Moon.

But every morn of woodbine fresh
  She made her garlanding,
And every night the dark glen Yew
  She wove, and she would sing.

And with her fingers, old and brown,
  She plaited Mats o' Rushes,
And gave them to the Cottagers
  She met among the Bushes.

Old Meg was brave as Margaret Queen,
  And tall as Amazon;
An old red blanket cloak she wore;
  A chip hat had she on.
God rest her aged bones somewhere –
  She died full long agone!

A Labourer

R. S. Thomas

Who can tell his years, for the winds have stretched
So tight the skin on the bare racks of bone
That his face is smooth, inscrutable as stone?
And when he wades in the brown bilge of earth
Hour by hour, or stoops to pull
The reluctant swedes, who can read the look
In the colourless eye, as his back comes straight
Like an old tree lightened of the snow's weight?
Is there love there, or hope, or any thought
For the frail form broken beneath his tread,
And the sweet pregnancy that yields his bread?

Gardener

Robert Graves

Loveliest flowers, though crooked in their border,
And glorious fruit, dangled from ill-pruned boughs –
Be sure the gardener had not eye enough
To wheel a barrow between the broadest gates
Without a clumsy scraping.

Yet none could think it simple awkwardness;
And when he stammered of a garden-guardian,
That the smooth lawns came by angelic favour,
The pinks and pears in spite of his own blunders,
They nudged at this conceit.

Well, he had something, though he called it nothing –
An ass's wit, a hairy-belly shrewdness
That would appraise the intentions of the angel
By the very difference of his own confusion,
And bring the most to pass.

The Vagabond

Robert Louis Stevenson

Give to me the life I love,
  Let the lave go by me,
Give the jolly heaven above
  And the by-way nigh me.
Bed in the bush with stars to see –
  Bread I dip in the river –
There's the life for a man like me,
  There's the life for ever.

Let the blow fall soon or late,
  Let what will be o'er me;
Give the face of earth around
  And the road before me.
Wealth I seek not, hope nor love,
  Nor a friend to know me;
All I seek, the heaven above
  And the road below me.

Or let autumn fall on me
  Where afield I linger,
Silencing the bird on tree,
  Biting the blue finger.
White as meal the frosty field –
  Warm the fireside haven –
Not to autumn will I yield,
  Not to winter even;

Let the blow fall soon or late,
  Let what will be o'er me;
Give the face of earth around
  And the road before me.
Wealth I ask not, hope nor love,
  Not a friend to know me.
All I ask, the heaven above,
  And the road below me.

The Ruined Maid

Thomas Hardy

'O 'melia, my dear, this does everything crown!
Who could have supposed I should meet you in Town?
And whence such fair garments, such prosperi-ty?' –
'O didn't you know I'd been ruined?' said she.

– 'You left us in tatters, without shoes or socks,
Tired of digging potatoes, and spudding up docks;
And now you've gay bracelets and bright feathers three!' –
'Yes: that's how we dress when we're ruined,' said she.

– 'At home in the barton you said "thee" and "thou",
And "thik oon", and "theäs oon", and "t'other"; but now
Your talking quite fits 'ee for high compa-ny!' –
'Some polish is gained with one's ruin,' said she.

– 'Your hands were like paws then, your face blue and bleak
But now I'm bewitched by your delicate cheek,
And your little gloves fit as on any la-dy!' –
'We never do work when we're ruined,' said she.

– 'You used to call home-life a hag-ridden dream,
And you'd sigh, and you'd sock; but at present you seem
To know not of megrims or melancho-ly!' –
'True. One's pretty lively when ruined,' said she.

– 'I wish I had feathers, a fine sweeping gown,
And a delicate face, and could strut about Town!' –
'My dear – a raw country girl, such as you be,
Cannot quite expect that. You ain't ruined,' said she.

Part Four

'Ensnared with Flowers'

'What wondrous life is this I lead!
Ripe apples drop about my head;
The luscious clusters of the vine
The nectarene, and curious peach,
Into my hands themselves do reach;
Stumbling on melons, as I pass,
Ensnared with flowers, I fall on grass.'

The Garden

Andrew Marvell

How vainly men themselves amaze
To win the palm, the oak, or bays,
And their uncessant labours see
Crowned from some single herb or tree,
Whose short and narrow vergèd shade
Does prudently their toils upbraid,
While all flow'rs and all trees do close
To weave the garlands of repose.

Fair Quiet, have I found thee here,
And Innocence, thy sister dear!
Mistaken long, I sought you then
In busy companies of men.
Your sacred plants, if here below,
Only among the plants will grow.
Society is all but rude,
To this delicious solitude.

No white nor red was ever seen
So am'rous as this lovely green.
Fond lovers, cruel as their flame,
Cut in these trees their mistress' name.
Little, alas, they know, or heed,
How far these beauties hers exceed!
Fair trees! wheres'e'er your barks I wound,
No name shall but your own be found.

When we have run our passion's heat,
Love hither makes his best retreat.
The gods, that mortal beauty chase,
Still in a tree did end their race.
Apollo hunted Daphne so,
Only that she might laurel grow.
And Pan did after Syrinx speed,
Not as a nymph, but for a reed.

What wondrous life is this I lead!
Ripe apples drop about my head;
The luscious clusters of the vine
Upon my mouth do crush their wine;
The nectarene, and curious peach,
Into my hands themselves do reach;
Stumbling on melons, as I pass,
Ensnared with flowers, I fall on grass.

Meanwhile the mind, from pleasures less,
Withdraws into its happiness:
The mind, that ocean where each kind
Does straight its own resemblance find,
Yet it creates, transcending these,
Far other worlds, and other seas,
Annihilating all that's made
To a green thought in a green shade.

Here at the fountain's sliding foot,
Or at some fruit-tree's mossy root,
Casting the body's vest aside,
My soul into the boughs does glide:
There like a bird it sits, and sings,
Then whets, and combs its silver wings;
And, till prepared for longer flight,
Waves in its plumes the various light.

Such was that happy garden-state,
While man there walked without a mate;
After a place so pure, and sweet,
What other help could yet be meet!
But 'twas beyond a mortal's share
To wander solitary there:
Two paradises 'twere in one
To live in paradise alone.

How well the skilful gardener drew
Of flowers and herbs this dial new,
Where from above the milder sun
Does through a fragrant zodiac run;
And, as it works, the industrious bee
Computes its time as well as we.
How could such sweet and wholesome hours
Be reckoned but with herbs and flowers!

A Garden Song

Henry Austin Dobson

Here, in this sequestered close,
Bloom the hyacinth and rose;
Here beside the modest stock
Flaunts the flaring hollyhock;
Here, without a pang, one sees
Ranks, conditions, and degrees.

All the seasons run their race
In this quiet resting place;
Peach, and apricot, and fig
Here will ripen, and grow big
Here is store and overplus, –
More had not Alcinous!

Here, in alleys cool and green,
Far ahead the thrush is seen;
Here along the southern wall
Keeps the bee his festival;
All is quiet else-afar
Sounds of toil and turmoil are.

Here be shadows large and long;
Here be spaces meet for song;
Grant, O garden-god, that I,
Now that mood and moment please, –
Find the fair Pierides!

from Maud

Alfred, Lord Tennyson

Come into the garden, Maud,
  For the black bat, night, has flown,
Come into the garden, Maud,
  I am here at the gate alone;
And the woodbine spices are wafted abroad,
  And the musk of the rose is blown.

For a breeze of morning moves,
   And the planet of Love is on high,
Beginning to faint in the light that she loves
   On a bed of daffodil sky,
To faint in the light of the sun she loves,
   To faint in his light, and to die.

All night have the roses heard
   The flute, violin, bassoon;
All night has the casement jessamine stirred
   To the dancers dancing in tune;
Till a silence fell with the waking bird,
   And a hush with the setting moon.

I said to the lily, 'There is but one
   With whom she has heart to be gay.
When will the dancers leave her alone?
   She is weary of dance and play.'
Now half to the setting moon are gone,
   And half to the rising day;
Low on the sand and loud on the stone
   The last wheel echoes away.

I said to the rose, 'The brief night goes
   In babble and revel and wine.
O young lord-lover, what sighs are those
   For one that will never be thine?
But mine, but mine,' so I sware to the rose,
   'For ever and ever, mine.'

And the soul of the rose went into my blood,
   As the music clashed in the hall;
And long by the garden lake I stood,
   For I heard your rivulet fall
From the lake to the meadow and on to the wood,
   Our wood, that is dearer than all;

From the meadow your walks have left so sweet
That whenever a March-wind sighs
He sets the jewel-print of your feet
In violets blue as your eyes,
To the woody hollows in which we meet
And the valleys of Paradise.

The slender acacia would not shake
One long milk-bloom on the tree;
The white lake-blossom fell into the lake,
As the pimpernel dozed on the lea;
But the rose was awake all night for your sake,
Knowing your promise to me;
The lilies and roses were all awake,
They sighed for the dawn and thee.

Queen rose of the rosebud garden of girls,
Come hither, the dances are done,
In gloss of satin and glimmer of pearls,
Queen lily and rose in one;
Shine out, little head, sunning over with curls
To the flowers, and be their sun.

There has fallen a splendid tear
From the passion-flower at the gate.
She is coming, my dove, my dear;
She is coming, my life, my fate;
The red rose cries, 'She is near, she is near;'
And the white rose weeps, 'She is late;'
The larkspur listens, 'I hear, I hear;'
And the lily whispers, 'I wait'.

She is coming, my own, my sweet;
Were it ever so airy a tread,
My heart would hear her and beat,
Were it earth in an earthy bed;
My dust would hear her and beat,
Had I lain for a century dead;
Would start and tremble under her feet,
And blossom in purple and red.

To the Small Celandine

William Wordsworth

Pansies, lilies, kingcups, daisies,
Let them live upon their praises;
Long as there's a sun that sets,
Primroses will have their glory;
Long as there are violets,
They will have a place in story:
There's a flower that shall be mine,
'Tis the little Celandine.

Ere a leaf is on a bush,
In the time before the thrush
Has a thought about her nest,
Thou wilt come with half a call,
Spreading out thy glossy breast
Like a careless Prodigal;
Telling tales about the sun,
When we've little warmth, or none.

from A Midsummer Night's Dream

William Shakespeare

I know a bank whereon the wild thyme blows,
Where ox-lips and the nodding violet grows;
Quite over-canopied with lush woodbine,
With sweet musk-roses, and with eglantine:
There sleeps Titania some time of the night,
Lull'd in these flowers with dances and delight;
And there the snake throws her enamell'd skin,
Weed wide enough to wrap a fairy in.

To Daffodils

Robert Herrick

Fair daffodils, we weep to see
You haste away so soon;
As yet the early-rising Sun
Has not attain'd his noon.
Stay, stay
Until the hasting day
Has run
But to the even song;
And, having pray'd together, we
Will go with you along.

We have short time to stay, as you,
We have as short a Spring;
As quick a growth to meet decay,
As you, or anything.
We die
As your hours do, and dry
Away
Like to the Summer's rain;
Or as the pearls of morning's dew,
Ne'er to be found again.

A Wish

Samuel Rogers

Mine be a cot beside the hill;
A bee-hive's hum shall soothe my ear;
A willowy brook that turns a mill,
With many a fall shall linger near.

The swallow, oft, beneath my thatch
Shall twitter from her clay-built nest;
Oft shall the pilgrim lift the latch,
And share my meal, a welcome guest.

Around my ivied porch shall spring
Each fragrant flower that drinks the dew;
And Lucy, at her wheel, shall sing
In russet-gown and apron blue.

The village-church among the trees,
Where first our marriage-vows were given,
With merry peals shall swell the breeze
And point with taper spire to Heaven.

I Bended unto Me

T.E. Brown

I bended unto me a bough of may,
That I might see and smell:
It bore it in a sort of way,
It bore it very well.
But when I let it backward sway,
Then it were hard to tell
With what a toss, with what a swing,
The dainty thing
Resumed its proper level,
And sent me to the devil.
I know it did – you doubt it?
I turned, and saw them whispering about it.

The Holly

Walter de la Mare

The sturdiest of forest-trees
With acorns is inset;
Wan white blossoms the elder brings
To fruit as black as jet;
But O, in all green English woods
Is aught so fair to view
As the sleek, sharp, dark-leaved holly tree
And its berries burning through?

Towers the ash; and dazzling green
The larch her tassels wears;
Wondrous sweet are the clots of may
The tangled hawthorn bears;
But O, in heath or meadow or wold
Springs aught beneath the blue
As brisk and trim as a holly-tree bole
With its berries burning through?

When hither, thither, falls the snow,
And blazes small the frost,
Naked amid the winter stars
The elm's vast boughs are tossed;
But O, of all that summer showed
What now to winter's true
As the prickle-beribbed dark holly tree,
With its berries burning through!

Loveliest of Trees

A.E. Housman

Loveliest of trees, the cherry now
Is hung with bloom along the bough,
And stands about the woodland ride
Wearing white for Eastertide.

Now, of my threescore years and ten,
Twenty will not come again,
And take from seventy springs a score,
It only leaves me fifty more.

And since to look at things in bloom
Fifty springs are little room,
About the woodlands I will go
To see the cherry hung with snow.

The Way Through the Woods

Rudyard Kipling

They shut the road through the woods
Seventy years ago.
Weather and rain have undone it again,
And now you would never know
There was once a road through the woods
Before they planted the trees.
It is underneath the coppice and heath,
And the thin anemones.
Only the keeper sees
That, where the ring-dove broods,
And the badgers roll at ease,
There was once a road through the woods.

Yet, if you enter the woods
Of a summer evening late,
When the night-air cools on the trout-ringed pools
Where the otter whistles his mate,
(They fear not men in the woods,
Because they see so few.)
You will hear the beat of a horse's feet,
And the swish of a skirt in the dew,
Steadily cantering through
The misty solitudes,
As though they perfectly knew
The old lost road through the woods . . .
But there is no road through the woods.

from Yardley Oak

William Cowper

Survivor sole, and hardly such, of all
That once liv'd here thy brethren, at my birth
(Since which I number three-score winters past)
A shatter'd veteran, hollow-trunk'd perhaps
As now, and with excoriate forks deform,
Relicts of ages! Could a mind, imbued
With truth from heav'n, created thing adore,
I might with rev'rence kneel and worship thee.
   It seems idolatry with some excuse
When our forefather Druids in their oaks
Imagin'd sanctity. The conscience yet
Unpurified by an authentic act
Of amnesty, the meed of blood divine,
Lov'd not the light, but gloomy into gloom
Of thickest shades, like Adam after taste
Of fruit proscrib'd, as to a refuge, fled.
   Thou wast a bauble once; a cup and ball,
Which babes might play with; and the thievish jay
Seeking her food, with ease might have purloin'd
The auburn nut that held thee, swallowing down
Thy yet close-folded latitude of boughs
And all thine embryo vastness, at a gulp.
But Fate thy growth decreed: autumnal rains
Beneath thy parent tree mellow'd the soil
Design'd thy cradle, and a skipping deer,
With pointed hoof dibbling the glebe, prepar'd
The soft receptacle in which secure
Thy rudiments should sleep the winter through.
   So Fancy dreams – Disprove it, if ye can,
Ye reas'ners broad awake, whose busy search

Of argument, employ'd too oft amiss,
Sifts half the pleasures of short life away.
Thou fell'st mature, and in the loamy clod
Swelling, with vegetative force instinct
Didst burst thine egg, as theirs the fabled Twins,
Now stars; two lobes, protruding, pair'd exact:
A leaf succeeded, and another leaf,
And all the elements thy puny growth
Fost'ring propitious, thou becam'st a twig.
Who liv'd when thou wast such? Oh couldst thou speak,
As in Dodona once thy kindred trees
Oracular, I would not curious ask
The future, best unknown, but at thy mouth
Inquisitive, the less ambiguous past.
By thee I might correct, erroneous oft,
The clock of history, facts and events
Timing more punctual, unrecorded facts
Recov'ring, and misstated setting right –
Desp'rate attempt, till trees shall speak again!
Time made thee what thou wast – King of the woods;
And Time hath made thee what thou art – a cave
For owls to roost in. Once thy spreading boughs
O'erhung the champain; and the numerous flock
That graz'd it stood beneath that ample cope
Uncrowded, yet safe-shelter'd from the storm.
No flock frequents thee now. Thou has outliv'd
Thy popularity and art become
(Unless verse rescue thee awhile) a thing
Forgotten, as the foliage of thy youth.
While thus through all the stages thou hast push'd
Of treeship, first a seedling hid in grass,
Then twig, then sapling, and, as century roll'd
Slow after century, a giant bulk
Of girth enormous, with moss-cushioned root
Upheav'd above the soil, and sides imboss'd
With prominent wens globose, till at the last
The rottenness, which Time is charg'd t' inflict
On other mighty ones, found also thee –
What exhibitions various hath the world
Witness'd of mutability in all
That we account most durable below!

Change is the diet, on which all subsist
Created changeable, and change at last
Destroys them. – Skies uncertain now the heat
Transmitting cloudless, and the solar beam
Now quenching in a boundless sea of clouds, –
Calm and alternate storm, moisture and drought,
Invigorate by turns the springs of life
In all that live, plant, animal, and man,
And in conclusion mar them. Nature's threads,
Fine passing thought, ev'n in her coarsest works,
Delight in agitation, yet sustain
The force that agitates, not unimpaired,
But, worn by frequent impulse, to the cause
Of their best tone their dissolution owe.
  Thought cannot spend itself, comparing still
The great and little of thy lot, thy growth
From almost nullity into a state
Of matchless grandeur, and declension thence
Slow into such magnificent decay.
Time was, when, settling on thy leaf, a fly
Could shake thee to the root – and time has been
When tempests could not. At thy firmest age
Thou hadst within thy bole solid contents
That might have ribb'd the sides or plank'd the deck
Of some flagg'd admiral; and tortuous arms,
The ship-wright's darling treasure, didst present
To the four-quarter'd winds, robust and bold,
Warp'd into tough knee-timber, many a load.
But the axe spar'd thee; in those thriftier days
Oaks fell not, hewn by thousands, to supply
The bottomless demands of contest wag'd
For senatorial honours. Thus to Time
The task was left to whittle thee away
With his sly scythe, whose ever-nibbling edge
Noiseless, an atom and an atom more
Disjoining from the rest, has, unobserv'd,
Achiev'd a labour, which had, far and wide,
(By man perform'd) made all the forest ring.

Part Five

'Beasts did Leap and Birds did Sing'

'As it fell upon a day
In the merry month of May,
Sitting in a pleasant shade,
Which a grove of myrtle made.
Beasts did leap and birds did sing.'

An Ode

Richard Barnfield

As it fell upon a day
In the merry month of May,
Sitting in a pleasant shade,
Which a grove of myrtles made.
Beasts did leap and birds did sing,
Everything did banish moan,
Save the nightingale alone.
She, poor bird, as all forlorn,
Lean'd her breast up-till a thorn,
And there sung the dolefull'st ditty
That to hear it was great pity.
Fie, fie, fie, now would she cry;
Tereu, tereu, by and by.

To the Cuckoo

William Wordsworth

O blithe New-comer! I have heard,
I hear thee and rejoice.
O Cuckoo! shall I call thee Bird,
Or but a wandering Voice?

While I am lying on the grass
Thy twofold shout I hear,
From hill to hill it seems to pass,
At once far off, and near.

Though babbling only to the Vale,
Of sunshine and of flowers,
Thou bringest unto me a tale
Of visionary hours.

Thrice welcome, darling of the Spring!
Even yet thou art to me
No bird, but an invisible thing,
A voice, a mystery;

The same whom in my school-boy days
I listened to; that Cry
Which made me look a thousand ways
In bush, and tree, and sky.

To seek thee did I often rove
Through woods and on the green;
And thou wert still a hope, a love;
Still longed for, never seen.

And I can listen to thee yet;
Can lie upon the plain
And listen, till I do beget
That golden time again.

O blessèd Bird! the earth we pace
Again appears to be
An unsubstantial, faery place;
That is fit home for Thee!

The Swallows

Andrew Young

All day – when early morning shone
With every dewdrop its own dawn
And when cockchafers were abroad
Hurtling like missiles that had lost their road –

The Swallows twisting here and there
Round unseen corners of the air
Upstream and down so quickly passed
I wondered that their shadows flew as fast.

They steeple-chased over the bridge
And dropped down to a drowning midge
Sharing the river with the fish,
Although the air itself was their chief dish.

Blue-winged snowballs! until they turned
And then with ruddy breasts they burned;
All in one instant everywhere,
Jugglers with their own bodies in the air.

To a Skylark

Percy Bysshe Shelley

Hail to thee, blithe Spirit!
Bird thou never wert,
That from heaven, or near it
Pourest thy full heart
In profuse strains of unpremeditated art.

Higher still and higher
From the earth thou springest
Like a cloud of fire;
The blue deep thou wingest,
And singing still dost soar, and soaring ever singest.

In the golden lightning
Of the sunken sun
O'er which clouds are brightening,
Thou dost float and run,
Like an embodied joy whose race is just begun.

The pale purple even
Melts around thy flight;
Like a star of heaven
In the broad daylight
Thou art unseen, but yet I hear thy shrill delight:

Keen as are the arrows
Of that silver sphere,
Whose intense lamp narrows
In the white dawn clear
Until we hardly see, we feel that it is there.

All the earth and air
With thy voice is loud,
As, when might is bare,
From one lonely cloud
The moon rains out her beams, and heaven is over-flow'd.

What thou art we know not;
What is most like thee?

From rainbow clouds there flow not
Drops so bright to see
As from thy presence showers a rain of melody.

Like a poet hidden
In the light of thought,
Singing hymns unbidden,
Till the world is wrought
To sympathy with hopes and fears it heeded not:

Like a high-born maiden
In a palace tower,
Soothing her love-laden
Soul in secret hour
With music sweet as love, which overflows her bower:

Like a glow-worm golden
In a dell of dew,
Scattering unbeholden
Its aerial hue
Among the flowers and grass, which screen it from the view:

Like a rose embower'd
In its own green leaves,
By warm winds deflower'd,
Till the scent it gives
Makes faint with too much sweet these heavy-winged thieves.

Sound of vernal showers
On the twinkling grass,
Rain-awaken'd flowers,

All that ever was
Joyous, and clear, and fresh, thy music doth surpass.

Teach us, sprite or bird,
What sweet thoughts are thine:
I have never heard
Praise of love or wine
That panted forth a flood of rapture so divine.

Chorus hymeneal
Or triumphal chaunt
Match'd with thine, would be all
But an empty vaunt –
A thing wherein we feel there is some hidden want.

What objects are the fountains
Of thy happy strain?
What fields, or waves, or mountains?
What shapes of sky or plain?
What love of thine own kind? what ignorance of pain?

With thy clear keen joyance
Languour cannot be:
Shadow of annoyance
Never came near thee:
Thou lovest; but ne'er knew love's sad satiety.

Waking or asleep
Thou of death must deem
Things more true and deep
Than we mortals dream,
Or how could thy notes flow in such a crystal stream?

We look before and after,
And pine for what is not:
Our sincerest laughter
With some pain is fraught;
Our sweetest songs are those that tell of saddest thought.

Yet if we could scorn
Hate, and pride, and fear;

If we were things born
Not to shed a tear,
I know not how thy joy we ever should come near.

Better than all measures
Of delightful sound,
Better than all treasures
That in books are found,
Thy skill to poet were, thou scorner of the ground!

Teach me half the gladness
That thy brain must know,
Such harmonious madness
From my lips would flow
The world should listen then, as I am listening now!

The Owl

Edward Thomas

Downhill I came, hungry, and yet not starved;
Cold, yet had heat within me that was proof
Against the North wind; tired, yet so that rest
Had seemed the sweetest thing under a roof.

Then at the inn I had food, fire, and rest,
Knowing how hungry, cold, and tired was I.
All of the night was quite barred out except
An owl's cry, a most melancholy cry

Shaken out long and clear upon the hill,
No merry note, nor cause of merriment,
But one telling me plain what I escaped
And other could not, that night, as in I went.

And salted was my food, and my repose,
Salted and sobered, too, by the bird's voice
Speaking for all who lay under the stars,
Soldiers and poor, unable to rejoice.

Owl

George Macbeth

is my favourite. Who flies
like a nothing through the night,
who-whoing. Is a feather
duster in leafy corners ring-a-rosy-ing
boles of mice. Twice

you hear him call. Who
is he looking for? You hear
him hovering over the floor
of the wood. O would you be gold
rings in the driving skull

if you could? Hooded and
vulnerable by the winter suns
owl looks. Is the grain of bark
in the dark. Round beaks are at
work in the pellety nest,

resting. Owl is an eye
in the barn. For a hole
in the trunk owl's blood
is to blame. Black talons in the
petrified fur! Cold walnut hands

on the case of the brain! In the reign
of the chicken owl comes like
a god. Is a goad in
the rain to the pink eyes,
dripping. For a meal in the day

flew, killed, on the moor. Six
mouths are the seed of his
arc in the season. Torn meat
from the sky. Owl lives
by the claws of his brain. On the branch

in the sever of the hand's
twigs owl is a backward look.
Flown wind in the skin. Fine
rain in the bones. Owl breaks
like the day. Am an owl, am an owl.

The Yellow-hammers

Andrew Young

All up the grassy many-tracked sheep-walk,
   Low sun on my right hand, hedge on my left
   Blotted by a late leaf, else leaf-bereft,
I drove my golden flock.

Yellow-hammers, gold-headed, russet-backed,
   They fled in jerky flight before my feet,
   Or pecked in the green ranks of winter-wheat,
While I my footsteps slacked.

Myself, the road, the hedge, these flying things,
   Who led, who followed as we climbed the hill?
   Loud as their repeated trembling trill-trill
Was the swift flirt of wings.

So tame I would have touched them with my hand,
   But they were gone, darting with rise and fall;
   I followed, till at the hedge-end they all
Dispersed over the land.

There, where the hill-side scattered the sheep-walk,
   Deserted by the birds I stood to muse
   How I but now had served so sweet a use,
Driving my golden flock.

THE DARKLING THRUSH

Thomas Hardy

I leant upon a coppice gate
   When Frost was spectre-gray,
And Winter's dregs made desolate
   The weakening eye of day.
The tangled bine-stems scored the sky
   Like strings of broken lyres,
And all mankind that haunted nigh
   Had sought their household fires.

The land's sharp features seemed to be
   The Century's corpse outleant,
His crypt the cloudy canopy,
   The wind his death-lament.
The ancient pulse of germ and birth
   Was shrunken hard and dry,
And every spirit upon earth
   Seemed fervourless as I.

At once a voice arose among
   The bleak twigs overhead
In a full-hearted evensong
   Of joy illimited;
An aged thrush, frail, gaunt, and small,
   In blast-beruffled plume,
Had chosen thus to fling his soul
   Upon the growing gloom.

So little cause for carollings
   Of such ecstatic sound
Was written on terrestrial things
   Afar or nigh around,
That I could think there trembled through
   His happy good-night air
Some blessed Hope, whereof he knew
   And I was unaware.

The Windhover: To Christ our Lord

Gerard Manley Hopkins

I caught this morning morning's minion, kingdom of daylight's
dauphin, dapple-dawn-drawn Falcon, in his riding
Of the rolling level underneath him steady air, and striding
High there, how he rung upon the rein of a wimpling wing
In his ecstasy! then off, off forth on swing,
As a skate's heel sweeps smooth on a bow-bend: the hurl and gliding
Rebuffed the big wind. My heart in hiding
Stirred for a bird, – the achieve of, the mastery of the thing!

Brute beauty and valour and act, oh, air, pride, plume, here
Buckle! AND the fire that breaks from thee then, a billion
Times told lovelier, more dangerous, O my chevalier!

No wonder of it: shéer plód makes plough down sillion
Shine, and blue-bleak embers, ah my dear,
Fall, gall themselves, and gash gold-vermilion.

The Hawk

George Mackay Brown

On Sunday the hawk fell on Bigging
And a chicken screamed
Lost in its own little snowstorm.
And on Monday he fell on the moor
And the Field Club
Raised a hundred silent prisms.
And on Tuesday he fell on the hill
And the happy lamb
Never knew why the loud collie straddled him.
And on Wednesday he fell on a bush
And the blackbird
Laid by his little flute for the last time.
And on Thursday he fell on Cleat
And peerie Tom's rabbit
Swung in a single arc from shore to hill.
And on Friday he fell on a ditch

But the rampant rat,
That eye and that tooth, quenched his flame.
And on Saturday he fell on Bigging
And Jock lowered his gun
And nailed a small wing over the corn.

The Chalk Blue Butterfly

Stephen Spender

The Chalk Blue (clinging to
A harebell stem, where it loops
Its curving wirefine neck
From which there hangs the flowerbell
Shaken by the wind that shakes
Too, the butterfly)
Opens now, now shuts, its wings,
Opening, shutting, on a hinge
Sprung at touch of sun or shadow.
   Open, the sunned wings mirror
Minute, double, all the sky.
   Shut, the ghostly underwing
Is cloud-opaque, bordered by
Copper spots embossed
With a goblin hammering.

   I look and look, as though my eyes
Could hold the Chalk Blue in a vice,
Waiting for some other witness –
That child's blue gaze, miraculous.
But today I am alone.

Flying Crooked

Robert Graves

The butterfly, a cabbage-white,
(His honest idiocy of flight)
Will never now, it is too late,
Master the art of flying straight,
Yet has – who knows so well as I? –
A just sense of how not to fly:
He lurches here and here by guess
And God and hope and hopelessness.
Even the aerobatic swift
Has not his flying-crooked gift.

To a Field-mouse

Robert Burns

Wee, sleekit, cow'rin', tim'rous beastie,
O what a panic's in thy breastie!
Thou need na start awa sae hasty,
Wi' bickering brattle!
I wad be laith to rin and chase thee
Wi' murd'ring pattle!

I'm truly sorry man's dominion
Has broken nature's social union,
An' justifies that ill opinion
Which makes thee startle
At me, thy poor earth-born companion,
An' fellow-mortal!

I doubt na, whyles, but thou may thieve;
What then? poor beastie, thou maun live!
A daimen icker in a thrave
'S a sma' request:
I'll get a blessin' wi' the lave,
And never miss 't!

Thy wee bit housie, too, in ruin!
Its silly wa's the win's are strewin':
And naething, now, to big a new ane,
O' foggage green!
And bleak December's winds ensuin'
Baith snell an' keen!

Thou saw the fields laid bare and waste
And weary winter comin' fast,
And cozie here, beneath the blast,
Thou thought to dwell,
Till, crash! The cruel coulter past
Out thro' thy cell.

That wee bit heap o' leaves an' stibble
Has cost thee mony a weary nibble!
Now thou's turn'd out, for a' thy trouble,
But house or hald,
To thole the winter's sleety dribble
An' cranreuch cauld!

But, Mousie, thou art no thy lane
In proving foresight may be vain:
The best laid schemes o' mice an' men
Gang aft a-gley,
An' lea'e us nought but grief an' pain,
For promised joy.

Still thou art blest, compared wi' me!
The present only toucheth thee:
But, och! I backward cast my e'e
On prospects drear!
An' forward, tho' I canna see,
I guess and fear!

Hedgehog

Anthony Thwaite

Twitching the leaves just where the drainpipe clogs
In ivy leaves and mud, a purposeful
Creature at night about its business. Dogs
Fear his stiff seriousness. He chews away

At beetles, worms, slugs, frogs. Can kill a hen
With one snap of his jaws, can taunt a snake
To death on muscled spines. Old countrymen
Tell tales of hedgehogs sucking a cow dry.

But this one, cramped by houses, fences, walls,
Must have slept here all winter in that heap
Of compost, or have inched by intervals
Through tidy gardens to this ivy bed.

And here, dim-eyed, but ears so sensitive
A voice within the house can make him freeze.
He scuffs the edge of danger; yet can live
Happily in our nights and absences.

A country creature, wary, quiet and shrewd,
He takes the milk we give him, when we're gone.
At night, our slamming voices must seem crude
To one who sits and waits for silences.

Hares at Play

John Clare

The birds are gone to bed the cows are still
And sheep lie panting on each old mole hill
And underneath the willows grey-green bough
Like toil a resting – lies the fallow plough
The timid hares throw daylights fears away
On the lanes road to dust and dance and play
Then dabble in the grain by nought deterred
To lick the dewfall from the barleys beard
Then out they sturt again and round the hill
Like happy thoughts dance squat and loiter still
Till milking maidens in the early morn
Gingle their yokes and start them in the corn
Through well known beaten paths each nimbling hare
Sturts quick as fear – and seeks its hidden lair.

Fox

Ted Hughes

Who
Wears the smartest evening dress in England?
Checks his watch by the stars
And hurries, white-scarfed,
To the opera
In the flea-ridden hen-house
Where he will conduct the orchestra?

Who
With a Robin Hood mask over his eyes
Meets King Pheasant the Magnificent
And with silent laughter
Shakes all the gold out of his robes
Then carries him bodily home
Over his shoulder,
A swag-bag?

And who
Flinging back his Dracula cloak
And letting one fang wink in the moonlight
Lifts off his top hat
Shows us the moon through the bottom of it
Then brings out of it, in a flourish of feathers,
The gander we locked up at sunset?

The Vixen

John Clare

Among the taller wood with ivy hung,
The old fox plays and dances round her young.
She snuffs and barks if any passes by
And swings her tail and turns prepared to fly.
The horseman hurries by, she bolts to see,
And turns agen, from danger never free.
If any stands she runs among the poles
And barks and snaps and drives them in the holes.
The shepherd sees them and the boy goes by
And gets a stick and progs the hole to try.
They get all still and lie in safety sure,
And out again when everything's secure,
And start and snap at blackbirds bouncing by
To fight and catch the great white butterfly.

The Combe

Edward Thomas

The Combe was ever dark, ancient and dark.
Its mouth is stopped with bramble, thorn, and briar;
And no one scrambles over the sliding chalk
By beech and yew and perishing juniper
Down the half precipices of its sides, with roots
And rabbit holes for steps. The sun of Winter,
The moon of Summer, and all the singing birds
Except the missel-thrush that loves juniper,
Are quite shut out. But far more ancient and dark
The Combe looks since they killed the badger there,
Dug him out and gave him to the hounds,
That most ancient Briton of English beasts.

A Runnable Stag

John Davidson

When the pods went pop on the broom, green broom
And apples began to be golden-skinned,
We harboured a stag in the Priory coomb,
And we feathered his trail up-wind, up-wind,
We feathered his trail up-wind –
A stag of warrant, a stag, a stag,
A runnable stag, a kindly crop,
Brow, bay and tray and three on top,
A stag, a runnable stag.

Then the huntsman's horn rang yap, yap, yap,
And 'Forwards' we heard the harbourer shout;
But 'twas only a brocket that broke a gap
In the beechen underwood, driven out,
From the underwood antlered out
By warrant and might of the stag, the stag,
The runnable stag, whose lordly mind
Was bent on sleep, though beamed and tined
He stood, a runnable stag.

So we tufted the covert till afternoon
With Tinkerman's Pup and Bell-of-the-North;
And hunters were sulky and hounds out of tune
Before we tufted the right stag forth,
Before we tufted him forth,
The stag of warrant, the wily stag,
The runnable stag with his kingly crop,
Brow, bay and tray and three on top,
The royal and runnable stag.

It was Bell-of-the-North and Tinkerman's Pup
  That stuck to the scent till the copse was drawn.
'Tally ho! tally ho!' and the hunt was up,
  The tufters whipped and the pack laid on,
  The resolute pack laid on,
    And the stag of warrant away at last,
    The runnable stag, the same, the same,
    His hoofs on fire, his horns like flame,
    A stag, a runnable stag.

'Let your gelding be: if you check or chide
  He stumbles at once and you're out of the hunt;
For three hundred gentlemen, able to ride,
  On hunters accustomed to bear the brunt,
  Accustomed to bear the brunt,
    Are after the runnable stag, the stag,
    The runnable stag with his kingly crop,
    Brow, bay and tray and three on top,
    The right, the runnable stag.'

By perilous paths in coomb and dell,
  The heather, the rocks, and the river-bed,
The pace grew hot, for the scent lay well,
  And a runnable stag goes right ahead,
  The quarry went right ahead –
    Ahead, ahead, and fast and far;
    His antlered crest, his cloven hoof,
    Brow, bay and tray and three aloof,
    The stag, the runnable stag.

For a matter of twenty miles and more,
  By the densest hedge and the highest wall,
Through herds of bullocks he baffled the lore
  Of harbourer, huntsmen, hounds and all,
  Of harbourer, hounds and all –
    The stag of warrant, the wily stag,
    For twenty miles, and five and five,
    He ran, and he never was caught alive,
    This stag, this runnable stag.

When he turned at bay in the leafy gloom,
  In the emerald gloom where the brook ran deep
He heard in the distance the rollers boom,
  And he saw in a vision of peaceful sleep.
  In a wonderful vision of sleep,
    A stag of warrant, a stag, a stag,
    A runnable stag in a jewelled bed,
    Under the sheltering ocean dead,
    A stag, a runnable stag.

So a fateful hope lit up his eye,
  And he opened his nostrils wide again,
And he tossed his branching antlers high
  As he headed the hunt down the Charlock glen,
  As he raced down the echoing glen,
    For five miles more, the stag, the stag,
    For twenty miles, and five and five,
    Not to be caught now, dead or alive,
    The stag, the runnable stag.

Three hundred gentlemen, able to ride,
  Three hundred horses as gallant and free,
Beheld him escape on the evening tide,
  Far out till he sank in the Severn Sea,
  Till he sank in the depths of the sea –
    The stag, the buoyant stag, the stag
    That slept at last in a jewelled bed
    Under the sheltering ocean spread.
    The stag, the runnable stag.

The Badger

John Clare

The badger grunting on his woodland track
With shaggy hide and sharp nose scrowed with black
Roots in the bushes and the woods and makes
A great hugh burrow in the ferns and brakes
With nose on ground he runs a awkard pace
And anything will beat him in the race
The shepherds dog will run him to his den

Followed and hooted by the dogs and men
The woodman when the hunting comes about
Go round at night to stop the foxes out
And hurrying through the bushes ferns and brakes
Nor see the many holes the badger makes
And often through the bushes to the chin
Breaks the old holes and tumbles headlong in.

When midnight comes a host of dogs and men
Go out and track the badger to his den
And put a sack within the hole and lye
Till the old grunting badger passes bye
He comes and hears they let the strongest loose
The old fox hears the noise and drops the goose
The poacher shoots and hurrys from the cry
And the old hare half wounded buzzes bye
They get a forked stick to bear him down
And clapt the dogs and bore him to the town
And bait him all the day with many dogs
And laugh and shout and fright the scampering hogs
He runs along and bites at all he meets
They shout and hollo down the noisey streets.

He turns about to face the loud uproar
And drives the rebels to their very doors
The frequent stone is hurled where ere they go
When badgers fight and every ones a foe
The dogs are clapt and urged to join the fray
The badger turns and drives them all away
Though scarcely half as big dimute and small
He fights with dogs for hours and beats them all
The heavy mastiff savage in the fray
Lies down and licks his feet and turns away
The bull dog knows his match and waxes cold
The badger grins and never leaves his hold
He drives the crowd and follows at their heels
And bites them through the drunkard swears and reels.

The frighted women takes the boys away
The blackguard laughs and hurrys on the fray
He tries to reach the woods a awkard race

But sticks and cudgels quickly stop the chace
He turns agen and drives the noisey crowd
And beats the many dogs in noises loud
He drives away and beats them every one
And then they loose them all and set them on
He falls as dead and kicked by boys and men
Then starts and grins and drives the crowd agen
Till kicked and torn and beaten out he lies
And leaves his hold and cackles groans and dies.

Some keep a baited badger tame as hog
And tame him till he follows like the dog
They urge him on like dogs and show fair play
He beats and scarcely wounded goes away
Lapt up as if asleep he scorns to fly
And siezes any dog that ventures nigh
Clapt like a dog he never bites the men
But worrys dogs and hurrys to his den
They let him out and turn a harrow down
And there he fights the host of all the town
He licks the patting hand and trys to play
And never trys to bite or run away
And runs away from noise in hollow trees
Burnt by the boys to get a swarm of bees.

At Grass

Philip Larkin

The eye can hardly pick them out
From the cold shade they shelter in,
Till wind distresses tail and mane;
Then one crops grass, and moves about
– The other seeming to look on –
And stands anonymous again.

Yet fifteen years ago, perhaps
Two dozen distances sufficed
To fable them: faint afternoons
Of Cups and Stakes and Handicaps,
Whereby their names were artificed
To inlay faded, classic Junes –

Silks at the start: against the sky
Numbers and parasols: outside,
Squadrons of empty cars, and heat,
And littered grass: then the long cry
Hanging unhushed till it subside
To stop-press columns on the street.

Do memories plague their ears like flies?
They shake their heads. Dusk brims the shadows.
Summer by summer all stole away,
The starting-gates, the crowds and cries –
All but the unmolesting meadows.
Almanacked, their names live; they

Have slipped their names, and stand at ease,
Or gallop for what must be joy,
And not a fieldglass sees them home,
Or curious stop-watch prophesies:
Only the groom, and the groom's boy,
With bridles in the evening come.

Bags of Meat

Thomas Hardy

'Here's a fine bag of meat,'
Says the master-auctioneer,
As the timid, quivering steer,
Starting a couple of feet
At the prod of a drover's stick,
And trotting lightly and quick,
A ticket stuck on his rump,
Enters with a bewildered jump.

'Where he's lived lately, friends,
I'd live till lifetime ends:
They've a whole life everyday
Down there in the Vale, have they!
He'd be worth the money to kill
And give away Christmas for goodwill.'

'Now here's a heifer – worth more
Than bid, were she bone-poor;
Yet she's round as a barrel of beer';
'She's a plum,' said the second auctioneer.

'Now this young bull – for thirty pound?
Worth that to manure your ground!'
'Or to stand,' chimed the second one,
'And have his picter done!'

The beast was rapped on the horns and snout
To make him turn about.
'Well,' cried a buyer, 'another crown –
Since I've dragged here from Taunton Town!'

'That calf, she sucked three cows,
Which is not matched for bouse
In the nurseries of high life
By the first-born of a nobleman's wife!'
The stick falls, meaning, 'A true tale's told,'
On the buttock of the creature sold,
And the buyer leans over and snips
His mark on one of the animal's hips.

Each beast, when driven in,
Looks round at the ring of bidders there
With a much-amazed reproachful stare,
As at unnatural kin,
For bringing him to a sinister scene
So strange, unhomelike, hungry, mean;
His fate the while suspended between
A butcher, to kill out of hand,
And a farmer, to keep on the land;
One can fancy a tear runs down his face
When the butcher wins, and he's driven from the place.

PART SIX

'The Swaying Sound of the Sea'

'Stand stable here
And silent be,
That through the channels of the ear
May wander like a river
The swaying sound of the sea.'

Seascape

W.H. Auden

Look, stranger, on this island now
The leaping light for your delight discovers,
Stand stable here
And silent be,
That through the channels of the ear
May wander like a river
The swaying sound of the sea.

Here at a small field's ending pause
When the chalk wall falls to the foam and its tall ledges
Oppose the pluck
And knock of the tide,
And the shingle scrambles after the sucking surf,
And a gull lodges
A moment on its sheer side.

Far off like floating seeds the ships
Diverge on urgent voluntary errands,
And this full view
Indeed may enter
And move in memory as now these clouds do,
That pass the harbour mirror
And all the summer through the water saunter.

After the Gale

Robert Bridges

Who has not walked upon the shore,
And who does not the morning know,
The day the angry gale is o'er,
The hour the wind has ceased to blow?

The horses of the strong south-west
Are pastured round his tropic tent,
Careless how long the ocean's breast
Sob on and sigh for passion spent.

The frightened birds, that fled inland
To house in rock and tower and tree,
Are gathering on the peaceful strand,
To tempt again the sunny sea;

Whereon the timid ships steal out
And laugh to find their foe asleep,
That lately scattered them about,
And drave them to the fold like sheep.

The snow-white clouds he northward chased
Break into phalanx, line, and band:
All one way to the south they haste,
The south, their pleasant fatherland.

From distant hills their shadows creep,
Arrive in turn and mount the lea,
And flit across the downs, and leap
Sheer off the cliff upon the sea;

And sail and sail far out of sight.
But still I watch their fleecy trains,
That piling all the south with light,
Dapple in France the fertile plains.

Break, Break, Break

Alfred, Lord Tennyson

Break, break, break,
   On thy cold grey stones, O Sea!
And I would that my tongue could utter
   The thoughts that arise in me.

O well for the fisherman's boy,
   That he shouts with his sister at play!
O well for the sailor lad,
   That he sings in his boat on the bay!

And the stately ships go on
   To their haven under the hill;
But O for the touch of a vanish'd hand,
   And the sound of a voice that is still!

Break, break, break,
   At the foot of thy crags, O Sea!
But the tender grace of a day that is dead
   Will never come back to me.

Sea Fever

John Masefield

I must down to the seas again, to the lonely sea and the sky,
And all I ask is a tall ship and a star to steer her by,
And the wheel's kick and the wind's song and the white sail's shaking,
And a grey mist on the sea's face and a grey dawn breaking.

I must down to the seas again, for the call of the running tide
Is a wild call and a clear call that may not be denied;
And all I ask is a windy day with the white clouds flying,
And the flung spray and the blown spume, and the sea-gulls crying.

I must down to the seas again, to the vagrant gipsy life,
To the gull's way and the whale's way where the wind's like a whetted knife;
And all I ask is a merry yarn from a laughing fellow-rover,
And quiet sleep and a sweet dream when the long trick's over.

from A Boy's Poem

Alexander Smith

The steamer left the black and oozy wharves,
And floated down between dark ranks of masts.
We heard the swarming streets, the noisy mills;
Saw sooty foundries full of glare and gloom,
Great bellied chimneys tipped by tongues of flame,
Quiver in smoky heat. We slowly passed
Loud building-yards, where every ship contained
A mighty vessel with a hundred men
Battering its iron sides. A cheer! a ship
In a gay flutter of innumerous flags
Slid gaily to her home. At length the stream
Broadened 'tween banks of daisies, and afar
The shadows flew upon the sunny hills;
And down the river, 'gainst the pale blue sky,
A town sat in its smoke. Look backward now!
Distance has stilled three hundred thousand hearts,
Drowned the loud roar of commerce, changed the proud
Metropolis which turns all things to gold,
To a thick vapour o'er which stands a staff
With smoky pennon streaming on the air.
Blotting the azure too, we floated on,
Leaving a long and weltering wake behind.
And now the grand and solitary hills
That never knew the toil and stress of man,
Dappled with sun and cloud, rose far away.
My heart stood up to greet the distant land
Within the hollows of whose mountains lochs
Moan in their restless sleep; around whose peaks,
And scraggy islands ever dim with rain,
The lonely eagle flies. The ample stream
Widened into a sea. The boundless day
Was full of sunshine and divinest light,
And far above the region of the wind
The barred and rippled cirrus slept serene,
With combed and winnowed streaks of faintest cloud
Melting into the blue.

Christmas at Sea

Robert Louis Stevenson

The sheets were frozen hard, and they cut the naked hand;
The decks were like a slide, where a seaman scarce could stand,
The wind was a nor'-wester, blowing squally off the sea;
And cliffs and spouting breakers were the only things a-lee.

They heard the surf a-roaring before the break of day;
But 'twas only with the peep of light we saw how ill we lay.
We tumbled every hand on deck instanter, with a shout,
And we gave her the maintops'l, and stood by to go about.

All day we tack'd and tack'd between the South Head and the North;
All day we haul'd the frozen sheets, and got no further forth;
All day as cold as charity, in bitter pain and dread,
For very life and nature we tack'd from head to head.

We gave the South a wider berth, for there the tide-race roar'd;
But every tack we made we brought the North Head close aboard;
So's we saw the cliffs and houses, and the breakers running high,
And the coastguard in his garden, with his glass against his eye.

The frost was on the village roofs as white as ocean foam;
The good red fires were burning bright in every 'longshore home;
The windows sparkled clear, and the chimneys volley'd out;
And I vow we sniff'd the victuals as the vessel went about.

The bells upon the church were rung with a mighty jovial cheer;
For it's just that I should tell you how (of all days in the year)
This day of our adversity was blessèd Christmas morn,
And the house above the coastguard's was the house where I was born.

O well I saw the pleasant room, the pleasant faces there,
My mother's silver spectacles, my father's silver hair;
And well I saw the firelight, like a flight of homely elves
Go dancing round the china-plates that stand upon the shelves!

And well I knew the talk they had, the talk that was of me,
Of the shadow on the household and the son that went to sea;
And O the wicked fool I seem'd, in every kind of way,
To be here and hauling frozen ropes on blessèd Christmas Day.

They lit the high sea-light, and the dark began to fall.
'All hands to loose topgallant sails!' I heard the captain call.
'By the Lord, she'll never stand it,' our first mate Jackson cried.
. . . 'It's the one way or the other, Mr Jackson,' he replied.

She stagger'd to her bearings, but the sails were new and good,
And the ship smelt up to windward just as though she understood.
As the winter's day was ending, in the entry of the night,
We clear'd the weary headland, and pass'd below the light.

And they heaved a mighty breath, every soul on board but me,
As they saw her nose again pointing handsome out to sea;
But all that I could think of, in the darkness and the cold,
Was just that I was leaving home and my folks were growing old.

The Inchcape Rock

Robert Southey

No stir in the air, no stir in the sea,
The ship was as still as she could be;
Her sails from heaven received no motion,
Her keel was steady in the ocean.

Without either sign or sound of their shock,
The waves flowed over the Inchcape Rock;
So little they rose, so little they fell,
They did not move the Inchcape bell.

The Abbot of Aberbrothok
Had placed that bell on the Inchcape Rock;
On a buoy in the storm it floated and swung,
And over the waves its warning rung.

When the rock was hid by the surge's swell,
The mariners heard the warning bell:
And then they knew the perilous rock,
And blessed the Abbot of Aberbrothok.

The sun in heaven was shining gay,
All things were joyful on that day;
The sea-birds screamed as they wheeled around,
And there was joyance in their sound.

The buoy of the Inchcape bell was seen,
A darker speck on the ocean green;
Sir Ralph the Rover walked his deck,
And he fixed his eye on the darker speck.

He felt the cheering power of spring,
It made him whistle, it made him sing;
His heart was mirthful to excess –
But the Rover's mirth was wickedness.

His eye was on the Inchcape float:
Quoth he, 'My men, put out the boat,
And row me to the Inchcape Rock,
And I'll plague the Abbot of Aberbrothok.'

The boat was lowered, the boatmen row,
And to the Inchcape Rock they go;
Sir Ralph bent over from the boat,
And he cut the bell from the Inchcape float.

Down sunk the bell with a gurgling sound –
The bubbles rose and burst around;
Quoth Sir Ralph, 'The next who comes to the Rock
Won't bless the Abbot of Aberbrothok.'

Sir Ralph the Rover sailed away;
He scoured the seas for many a day;
And, now grown rich with plundered store,
He steers his course for Scotland's shore.

So thick a haze o'erspreads the sky
They cannot see the sun on high;
The wind hath blown a gale all day,
At evening it hath died away.

On the deck the Rover takes his stand,
So dark it is they see no land.
Quoth Sir Ralph, 'It will be lighter soon,
For there is the dawn of the rising moon.'

'Canst hear', said one, 'the breakers roar?
For methinks we should be near the shore.
Now where we are we cannot tell,
But I wish I could hear the Inchcape bell.'

They hear no sound – the swell is strong;
Though the wind hath fallen they drift along
Till the vessel strikes with a shivering shock –
'Oh! heavens! it is the Inchcape Rock!'

Sir Ralph the Rover tore his hair,
And curst himself in his despair:
The waves rush in on every side,
The ship is sinking beneath the tide.

But even in his dying fear,
One dreadful sound could the Rover hear –
A sound as if, with the Inchcape bell,
The Devil below was ringing his knell.

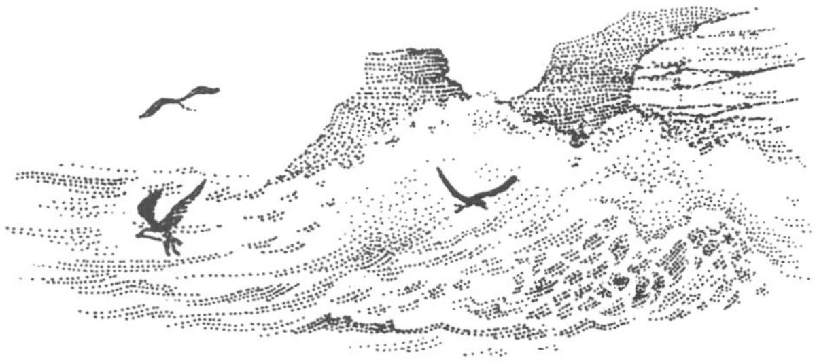

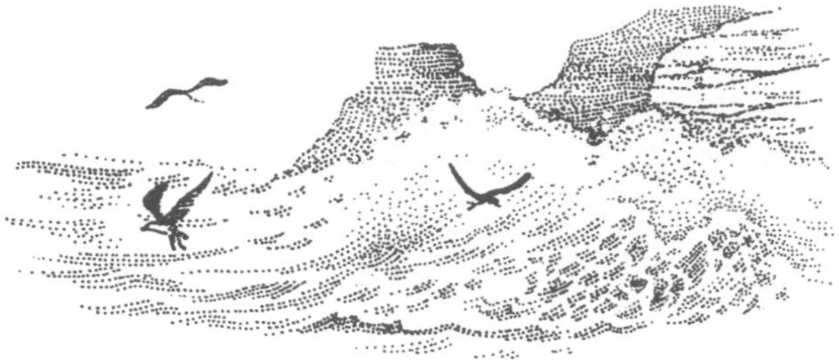

The Coastwise Lights

Rudyard Kipling

Our brows are bound with spindrift and the weed is on our knees;
Our loins are battered 'neath us by the swinging, smoking seas.
From reef and rock and skerry – over headland, ness, and voe –
The Coastwise Lights of England watch the ships of England go!

Through the endless summer evenings, on the lineless, level floors;
Through the yelling Channel tempest when the siren hoots and roars –
By day the dipping house-flag and by night the rocket's trail –
As the sheep that graze behind us so we know them where they hail.

We bridge across the dark, and bid the helmsman have a care,
The flash that, wheeling inland, wakes his sleeping wife to prayer.
From our vexed eyries, head to gale, we bind in burning chains
The lover from the sea-rim drawn – his love in English lanes.

We greet the clippers wing-and-wing that race the Southern wool;
We warn the crawling cargo-tanks of Bremen, Leith, and Hull;
To each and all our equal lamp at peril of the sea –
The white wall-sided warships or the whalers of Dundee!

Come up, come in from Eastward, from the guardports of the Morn!
Beat up, beat in from Southerly, O gipsies of the Horn!
Swift shuttles of an Empire's loom that weave us main to main,
The Coastwise Lights of England give you welcome back again!

Go, get you gone up-Channel with the sea-crust on your plates;
Go, get you into London with the burden of your freights!
Haste, for they talk of Empire there, and say, if any seek,
The Lights of England sent you and by silence shall ye speak!

Ye Mariners of England

Thomas Campbell

Ye Mariners of England
That guard our native seas!
Whose flag has braved, a thousand years,
The battle and the breeze!
Your glorious standard launch again
To match another foe:
And sweep through the deep,
While the stormy winds do blow;
While the battle rages loud and long
And the stormy winds do blow.

The spirits of your fathers
Shall start from every wave –
For the deck it was their field of fame,
And Ocean was their grave:
Where Blake and mighty Nelson fell
Your manly hearts shall glow,
As ye sweep through the deep,
While the stormy winds do blow;
While the battle rages loud and long
And the stormy winds do blow.

Britannia needs no bulwarks,
No towers along the steep;
Her march is o'er the mountain-waves,
Her home is on the deep.
With thunders from her native oak
She quells the floods below –
As they roar on the shore,
When the stormy winds do blow;
When the battle rages loud and long,
And the stormy winds do blow.

The meteor flag of England
Shall yet terrific burn;
Till danger's troubled night depart
And the star of peace return.
Then, then, ye ocean-warriors!
Our song and feast shall flow
To the fame of your name,
When the storm has ceased to blow;
When the fiery fight is heard no more,
And the storm has ceased to blow.

Index of Colour Plates

Index of Authors

Index of First Lines

Acknowledgements

PHOTOGRAPHS

Bruce Coleman Ltd: Jane Burton 6, Jill E. Burton 54, Erich Crichton 66, 111. L.R. Dawson 134, P.A. Hinchliffe 127, Hans Reinhard 114, 130, Kim Taylor 123; John Glover 11, 27, 98; Impact Photos: Mark Cator 91, Roger Perry 43, Pamela Toler 23, 103; S. & O. Matthews 70, 78, 94; The Photographers' Library 2–3, 30, 62, 75, 147; Seaphot Ltd/ Planet Earth Pictures: J.G. James 19, Andrew Mounter 150, Keith Scholey 35, Philip Smith 142.

POEMS

Grateful acknowledgement is made to the following publishers, authors, and other copyright holders, for permission to reprint copyrighted material. While every effort has been made to obtain permission for the publication of all copyright material it is possible that we may inadvertently have failed to obtain the necessary permission. In all cases we offer our apologies to the copyright holders.

Faber and Faber Ltd for 'On this Island' (Seascape) from *Collected Poems* by W.H. Auden; John Murray (Publishers) Ltd for 'A Bay in Anglesey' and 'Trebetherick' from *Collected Poems* by Sir John Betjeman; A.D. Peters & Co. Ltd for 'The Mole Catcher' from *Poems of Many Years* by Edmund Blunden; The Hogarth Press for 'The Hawk' from *The Year of the Whale* by George Mackay Brown; The Literary Trustees of Walter de la Mare and The Society of Authors as their representatives for 'Snow' and 'The Holly' by Walter de la Mare; The author for 'Flying Crooked' and 'Gardener' from *Collected Poems 1975* by Robert Graves; The Society of Authors as the literary representative of the Estate of A.E. Housman and Jonathan Cape Ltd for 'Loveliest of Trees' from *Collected Poems* by A.E. Housman; Faber and Faber Ltd for 'Pennines in April' from *Lupercal* and 'Fox' from *What is the Truth?* by Ted Hughes; The National Trust for Places of Historic Interest or Natural Beauty and Macmillan London Ltd for 'Sussex', 'The Way through the Woods' and 'The Coastwise Lights' from *The Definitive Edition of Rudyard Kipling's Verse*; Marvell Press for 'At Grass' from *The Less Deceived* by Philip Larkin; Mrs Valda Grieve and Martin Brian & O'Keefe Ltd for 'Scotland Small?' by Hugh MacDiarmid; The Society of Authors as the literary representative of the Estate of John Masefield for 'Up on the Downs', 'The Waggon-Maker' and 'Sea Fever' by John Masefield; Faber and Faber Ltd for 'Zennor' from *The Nine Bright Shiners* by Anne Ridler; Faber and Faber Ltd for 'The Chalk Blue Butterfly' from *The Generous Days* by Stephen Spender; David Higham Associates Ltd for 'Fern Hill' and 'Poem in October' from *Collected Poems* by Dylan Thomas; Grafton Books, A Division of the Collins Publishing Group, for 'The Welsh Hill Country' and 'A Labourer' from *Song at the Year's Turning* by R.S. Thomas. The author for 'Hedgehog' from *Poems 1953–1983* (published by Martin Secker & Warburg Ltd) by Anthony Thwaite; Martin Secker & Warburg Ltd for 'The Yellow Hammers' and 'The Swallows' from *The Poetical Works of Andrew Young*.